Receiving praise from a student is the highest form of compliment for me. When I was guided to become a teacher, I was initially overwhelmed by the responsibility. However, whenever I have a new client, I feel nervous and excited about the meeting because it's the most important thing in my life that day. I am equally thrilled to have a one-on-one session as I am to speak in front of a large audience. It's all similarly rewarding and meaningful work that I am grateful to be able to do.
With an open heart and a kind soul,
Gina.

What People Are Saying About

Planet Walking...

For me, the best part is Gina's moving story of dead-ends and discoveries. Going through many different trials and challenges. A good story is usually better than advice and recommendations. You find inspiring narratives in ancient myths and fairy tales where the main character has to find a way through impossible ordeals. If the story is true to life and ancient, it comes from deep in the human soul. Gina's story is heartfelt, open and complicated. She tells it in a way that you feel her passions and her disappointments. In the end, you are relieved that she found her way back into life.

I suggest reading Gina's story more than once to notice the subtle details that can offer you guidance. Don't feel alone. Your path has been walked before, and the seasoned survivors know a thing or two about it. Her narrative may help you sort out your own, and you have to find ways to alter it toward hope.

Thomas Moore, Psychotherapist, Buddhist, Spiritual Teacher, Foreword from *Surviving Suicidal Ideation* (Cavalier's previous book)

I have been on a spiritual journey for the past five years, learning, consuming, and growing as much as possible. Gina Cavalier has been a pillar of hope for me in this journey and a guiding light when things become confusing. And believe me, things can become confusing. There is a wealth of information on spiritual practice, each with its own nuance but many with the same roots. The most challenging part of the journey has been figuring out how to read my spiritual map, understand my body and intuition, and know when to turn right, left, or rest at the crossroads. *Planet Walking* is the beacon

of light at the end of a confusing maze. It's a wonderfully written guide for those of us who want to know more but need a well-structured map of how to consume this information in a way that works and manifests. There are so many concepts to understand that searching for clues in hundreds of different sources can become overwhelming. In *Planet Walking, A Handbook for the Living,* Gina deftly lays out everything you need to know for your journey with proper expertise and loving kindness. I work with Gina as my spiritual mentor, and this book is the actual manuscript of all she has taught me. It's a beautiful reference guide, an incredible journey if you are new to spirituality, and an adventure if you are open to "more." May you find your way, as I found mine, through this easy-to-understand guide written by a beautiful human who truly understands the human spirit.
Dr. Jeanne Retief, PhD

When I first embarked on my spiritual journey, I felt overwhelmed by the number of options and directions I could take in finding my path. It was difficult navigating my human existence, let alone the myriads of information regarding spirituality ... I had no idea where to begin. Then, the universe sent me Gina. She became my spiritual mentor (mama), helping me find my way home to my spirit in this human world. Gina has a gift for gently taking your hand and guiding you toward what you are ready to learn, receive, and integrate into your life. Through *Planet Walking*, her mentorship is accessible to anyone prepared to begin their journey. If you are ready to connect deeply with your spirit and walk your divine path, Gina will guide you just as she has done for many others. May it be filled with love, light, and blessings!
Linnea Hodson, Mentee, The Liberated Healer

Planet Walking, a Handbook for the Living

A 6-Week Healing Program for Liberation and Specific Guidance on Suicidal Ideation

Also by This Author

Surviving Suicidal Ideation: From Therapy to Spirituality and the Lived Experience
ISBN: 978-0877853657

Gina Cavalier's — How I Became Santa Claus
ISBN: 0990565904

Copyright Information & Previous Book

First Edition, 2024

ISBN: 978-0877853657 – *Surviving Suicidal Ideation: From Therapy to Spirituality and the Lived Experience*

Some content originally appeared in the following publications and is used here with permission from The Swedenborg Foundation: Cavalier, Gina, and Amelia Kelley. *Surviving Suicidal Ideation*. Royersford: Swedenborg Foundation, 2024: Thomas Moore's endorsement/foreword, Commitment image on page 2, Chakra Images body, hands and feet pages 157–160, Angel and White Horse Image on page 186, I am Joy Meditation page 204, artwork page 25, Zipper Meditation page 71, Meditation page 75, Morning and Evening Practice page 17, Safety Plan, Resources 212–215.

Planet Walking, a Handbook for the Living

A 6-Week Healing Program for Liberation and Specific Guidance on Suicidal Ideation

Gina Cavalier

BOOKS

London, UK

Washington, DC, USA

CollectiveInk

First published by O-Books, 2025
O-Books is an imprint of Collective Ink Ltd.,
Unit 11, Shepperton House, 89 Shepperton Road, London, N1 3DF
office@collectiveinkbooks.com
www.collectiveinkbooks.com
www.o-books.com

For distributor details and how to order please visit the 'Ordering' section on our website.

ISBN: 978 1 80341 833 9
978 1 80341 963 3 (ebook)
Library of Congress Control Number: 2024945963

A CIP catalogue record for this book is available from the British Library.

Design: Lapiz Digital Services

UK: Printed and bound by CPI Group (UK) Ltd, Croydon, CR0 4YY
Printed in North America by CPI GPS partners

The author of this book does not dispense medical advice or prescribe the use of any technique as a form of treatment for physical, emotional, or medical problems without the advice of a physician, either directly or indirectly. The intent of the author is only to offer information of a general nature to help you in your quest for emotional and spiritual well-being. In the event you use any of the information in this book for yourself, which is your constitutional right, the author and the publisher assume no responsibility for your actions.

Contents

Messages

Why?

Eighty percent of people can't get help from their insurance, mental health programs, or other sources, so we are trying every way we can to create more materials to help people.

This Is Not Just a Journal

This program has been successfully taught to numerous clients over many years and has now been organized into a comprehensive system. The program aims to help individuals understand and navigate the energy of the planet, providing guidance and messages for people dealing with various mental health and emotional challenges, including suicidal thoughts. By following this day-by-day process, you will notice tangible changes in your life as you start to sense, feel, hear, and understand that transformation is taking place. Embracing the energy of the planet rather than resisting it is critical to this process.

Spiritual Message to You

Start small, just like all gardens. If you plant the seeds in the right direction and give them the proper nutrients, you'll witness your life blooming in ways that fulfill your highest purpose. Spiritual practice is focused on realizing the truth and achieving liberation from the cycle of birth and death. Devotion, surrender, and selfless service are essential for attaining spiritual realization. We express gratitude for the blessings and energies that support our journey. Thank you for loving yourself enough to embark on this journey and trusting the process with love, which is the most extraordinary energy of all.

Teacher

True teachers never stop learning, but they have reached a point where they have studied and mastered a level of tools and practiced a way to communicate those tools in a way that is beneficial to a student. They are "in-service" to raising a community. All teachers are this way, and we need to shift away from praising those who are not in service to humanity and instead place it more on those who make these sacrifices. It is a sacrifice but a soul-rewarding one. Many people claim to be teachers, and they can do more damage than good, which can be hard to spot. I've recently found a young, beautiful girl online who poses herself as an Earth Angel/Star Seed (we are all star seeds, by the way!) and all-knowing. Still, it is all about her unique journey, and she puts herself above others; this is not the role of a real Planet Walking teacher.

Here is a quick way to determine if you are trying to decide if someone is not authentic in this area. They put themselves on a pedestal higher than others. They tend to overuse the word I. Yes, we all come here with specific gifts, and you will find yours in this book. There is a period when you are the student, and at one point, you can become a teacher, but the words should feel like WE!

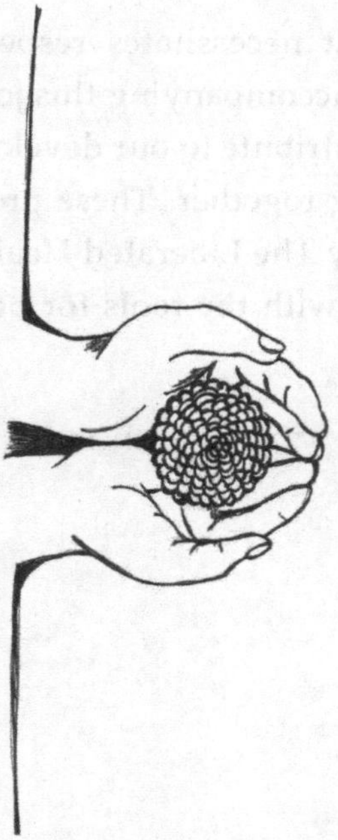

THE ENERGY OF "WE"
Open and Gentle

THE ENERGY OF "I"
Closed and Controlled

Reader

As we journey through life, we can perceive our existence as a vast classroom where every experience is a profound lesson. This broader perspective allows us to transcend the confines of the self and embrace a collective consciousness. By recognizing ourselves as boundless entities, we can navigate through any circumstance gracefully. Throughout our lives, we continuously assume the role of both student and teacher. It is essential to remain receptive to the guiding influence of those who impact our lives, as this forms the foundation of the student-teacher relationship. Eventually, as we integrate these lessons, we may transition into mentors ourselves, unlocking further spiritual growth and learning. However, this transition has complexities and demands integrity, ethical conduct, and equilibrium. Embracing student and teacher roles is a transformative and enriching aspect of life, but it necessitates respect and acknowledgment of the challenges accompanying this journey. Let us honor all individuals who contribute to our development and recognize the value of evolving together. These profound insights and teachings are crafted by The Liberated Healer™, a framework that equips individuals with the tools for personal growth and healing.

Dedication

"The Garden of Souls"

This book is dedicated to all those souls who have passed away from any form of suicide in their journey. Santa Muerte brings roses, the universal symbol of love, to assist us in our soul's healing journey and to always come back to love, our most authentic nature as a human walking this wonderous Planet.

SANTA MUERTE, the love of 100,000 mothers, would never condone hurting another soul

The spiritual guides have advised that we rename Purgatory, as it does not accurately reflect its true nature. It is instead a place of purification; it is a serene and beautiful garden filled with compassion and love. From now on, we will refer to this place as "The Garden of Souls," a place that represents every soul that has passed from Suicide and a sanctuary for them to rest. These souls hold a sacred space for their fellow humans with profound love and prayers, hoping others do not have to depart similarly unless their soul wants that experience. Their presence will always be felt in "The Garden of Souls," which energetically holds space for us with an understanding of how hard these lessons of life can be, but with support, we can climb above the mud to our salvation.

I wish to manifest this in physical locations positioned globally where humans can reflect, meditate, and find solace to process life's emotions with the support of the "Garden of Souls."

We aspire to establish one of the first "Garden of Souls" in the United States as a serene sanctuary to honor and remember those who have departed. This visionary space will resemble a park, providing a place for people to meditate, find solace, and connect with the spirits of their loved ones. Skilled architects will meticulously design the garden, focusing on the rose as a symbol of beauty and remembrance.

This meaningful project was inspired by a powerful message conveyed through a long-standing connection with a shaman who has worked alongside Gina for over two decades. Santa Muerte, the revered lady of Holy Death, brought forth a new perspective on addressing suicide, compelling us to consider alternative ways to save souls. She shared the vision of the "Garden of Souls," a spiritual manifestation we are eager to bring to life in the physical realm. This sacred garden will provide a refuge for humanity to pay tribute to and provide support for those who have departed, fostering unity and empathy within our communities. A radiant rose will symbolize each soul, and our collective love will guide them beyond the suffering they endured in life. We intend to grant them liberation, breaking down any barriers they may have erected around themselves. This tranquil garden will offer them peace and comfort, allowing them solace and serenity. We are calling out to those in high places and governments to help us create this space for us to heal and ponder, something we are missing and should be in cities so this can be a refuge for those who need to reset.

Santa Muerte has been given, in some senses, a bad rap because she has been called forth and conjured to help souls in an Earthly war of karma. She represents such deep love that she carries the love of 100,000 mothers. She could never hurt another soul and is not revengeful in any way, which is why she comes to selected Earth-bound channels and shamans. Many of these terms will be explored in the following text.

We sing the words guided by Santa Muerte with thanks and grace:

We are so precious; everyone is so precious; our lives here on Earth are so precious; everything connected to us is so precious; sending energy to everyone is so precious; praying for healing suicidal ideation in those you love is so precious; you are so precious.

Disclaimers & Trigger Warnings

Trigger Warnings: The author of this book wants to emphasize that they are not a medical or mental health professional, nor do they claim to have any specific certifications. The content of this book has the potential to bring up strong emotions and can impact your past experiences, belief systems, and religious understandings in various ways. It is strongly recommended that you consult with your medical or religious advisors in conjunction with reading this book or in any area where you may require assistance. It is essential to recognize that only you can determine if you are ready to engage with and work through this information. If you feel this book is unsuitable, please understand that this is not the author or publisher's intention, and you should not blame yourself. It is essential to approach this material with a heightened awareness of your mental and emotional state.

Please Understand: Due to the sensitive nature of the subject matter, we have been advised to include the following disclaimer to protect everyone involved in this critical project. It is essential to be cautious about anything that might be triggering and to move away from any material that feels uncomfortable. Some people may choose to read through the book in order, while others may prefer to select topics and exercises that resonate with them at that time. There is no universally correct approach — everyone should choose what feels right. We are also including a safety plan so you can either keep it for personal use or share it with others.

The Author: Please note that parts of this work are based on the author's personal experiences with suicidal ideation and her research into seeking healing therapies, practitioners, and modalities to help stop and manage her suicidal thoughts. It's important to understand that her opinions, expressions, and experiences may not be suitable for the public or individuals with specific diagnoses. Readers should be aware that they assume their risks, and the author of this content holds no liability for its use.

Important Notice: This book is intended to provide information and education about psychological topics. However, it is crucial to remember that it does not replace the need for consulting a licensed medical or mental health professional. The readers and their advocates are strongly advised to regularly consult with a physician or mental health professional to address any health concerns, especially those requiring diagnosis or medical attention. It is essential to seek approval from a medical professional familiar with your medical history or that of your loved one before starting any new medication, therapy, or alternative treatments. By reading this book, you indicate your acceptance of this disclaimer.

Might Not Resonate for You: While the book aims to provide support for individuals struggling with thoughts of suicide or coping with the aftermath of suicide, it's important to note that the content may not necessarily connect with everyone. The thoughts and opinions in the book may or may not align with your experiences or beliefs. If any part of the book doesn't resonate with you, it's okay only to take away the helpful parts and leave the rest behind. By reading this book, you indicate your acceptance of this disclaimer and hold the author and the publisher harmless as you make your own decisions.

Introduction

You are the JOY that nothing else is. Your SOUL is the most valuable thing you own.
Take care of it.

– Gina Cavalier

The Vision & Goal

Many of the practices in this book will be listed at www.theliberatedhealer.com, www.ginacavalier.com, and on our YouTube channel @LoveandMedia.

Introducing *Planet Walking, A Handbook for the Living: A 6-Week Healing Program for Liberation and Specific Guidance on Suicidal Ideation*. This essential book provides comprehensive guidance for those looking to heal using energy and spiritual tools taught at the Liberated Healer™. Labor with love is bliss; I am lucky to be here with you. Thank you.

The book is about love and how to live in this vibration more, which is our most authentic self and how we came into the world at birth – all of us, even those you feel and think are so different from ourselves. Whenever you feel challenged by the text or exercises, please try to lean into love. If something is not resonating, let it go and move more towards love. This is a simple handbook to guide those seeking to explore the Planet, awaken, become conscious, and gain tools to heal themselves from mental, emotional, physical, and spiritual illnesses. All humans attach a wide variety of emotions to the word love, but the universal love vibration encircles the entire planet Earth (the Earth's aura). It has no emotion related to love; it just is. It's the reason many people who feel suicidal say, "I want to go home." Because the love here is dense and rooted in emotion, and we can feel heavy with it, this book aims to help you lighten that feeling on your own. It gives you the tools to get back to who you are, and Planet Walk enjoying each experience as a gift curated just for you.

Remember, you have 50 trillion cells, each holding energy and a function for us to live. This is a practice and a way of life. Be gentle with yourself as you proceed.

The goal is to gain a deep understanding of the value of your soul and your life's purpose so you can confidently move towards living the life you prefer. This was our truest nature initially, but with our modern times, cement, conflicts, use of plastics, chemicals, Wi-Fi, and technologies such as radio frequencies moving through our system, we have lost some of our natural knowingness, knowledge, and capabilities. This will help uncover the true meaning of your allotted time on this wondrous Planet Earth. You will gain an understanding of universal light, shadow, and dark language, and how the energies all work together to grow and evolve your soul. Understand that each interaction has been perfectly orchestrated so you can find ways to liberate yourself, your knowledge, healing, and how you impact others. This information is coming into the world now, as we need as many souls as possible to awaken to these gifts faster, with more clarity, as we have entered the "Age of Aquarius." Those souls who felt disconnected, numb, and lost and considered such extreme thoughts as suicidal ideation and other mental health struggles (some conditions might need therapeutic assistance with trained medical professionals alongside these techniques) will understand why they are so sensitive. It's not the desire to leave their physical body but the dense energies and identities they are trying to process. Through this program and gaining this understanding, you will start to regain seniority in this life with strength, knowing how powerful you are, and it will become harder to hold a thought of self-harm, as well as hurting others because you will become the most valuable thing you own. Would you throw a million dollars in the trash? Probably not, and now you will see that you are just as valuable, and thus, with this knowing, you will change, and along with it, the world will change around you. This is the place to start if we want a kinder world, one day free of the treacherous things made by horror films. One day, a utopia, but it must begin with you.

The Five Foundational Practices

I. The importance of self-awareness and self-love — Embracing others and their role in our learning journey.
II. Embracing Others — Viewing everyone and everything as a teacher — Letting go of the desire to win over others — Needing to be correct — The impact of understanding on conflicts and wars.
III. Embracing Challenges — Understanding the purpose of challenging experiences as lessons to help you and others grow — The pain that has been placed on you, you might have put on others in one way at this time or in another — we are all complicit — Embracing personal growth and spiritual development.
IV. Fulfilling Your Soul's Lesson Plan — Uncovering personal gifts and life's purpose — Relentless pursuit of personal fulfillment and self-discovery.
V. Connection to All Living Things — Recognizing the essence of all creation — Embracing learning and growth with neutrality and excitement.

Who Is This Book For?

I. The world is filled with individuals who are facing a myriad of challenges and obstacles. It's essential not to pass judgment on their experiences but to extend a helping hand to guide them toward a brighter future. Throughout our struggles, there are opportunities for growth and learning.

II. If you feel disconnected from your true purpose or need more enthusiasm, this book has been crafted and created exceptionally to guide you. It serves as a proactive guidebook, offering valuable insights to help you navigate through life and rediscover your sense of purpose and, primarily, self-love.

III. Perhaps you are a curious adventurer eager to delve into the workings of energy. While you may possess some comprehension of these intricate concepts, you yearn to deepen your understanding of our interconnectedness within the universe and energetic realms. You desire to comprehend the unique language and rhythm of your soul. You want to feel safe in your learning and not get pulled into groups with hidden agendas to use your energy for their benefit. This book puts you in the driver's seat of all that is you.

IV. Or maybe you are here seeking ways to aid a struggling loved one, hoping to grasp insights that can offer support. Your dedication is commendable, and we wish you to uncover valuable guidance within this book and, in turn, discover personal solace.

V. For those of you grappling with the emotional fallout of a loss due to suicide, you seek understanding and healing. We hope that within these pages, you find solace, knowledge, and a path toward healing as we acknowledge your pain and stand beside you with empathy and understanding. Healing becomes a personal journey, and it's our collective hope to halt the recurrence of such devastating acts.

1975 Cavalier Family (Ages: Gina 5, Johnny 9, Patricia 30, Gino 41)

A Child's Heart Hurts Without Healing

In my first coauthored book, *Surviving Suicidal Ideation: From Therapy to Spirituality and the Lived Experience,* I share the deeply personal journey of overcoming abuse and neglect that led me to contemplate suicide. I delve into the transformative healing process, addressing emotional wounds and physical ailments. Through this practice, I aim to convey that we all deserve the ability to manifest the lives we envision. We are all worthy of love and safety, and we need to start demanding it in our world as wounded children become wounded adults, and they are only mimicking what they are learning. If not for yourself as a tribe, can we not do it for the world's children? Maybe we can all get inspired to make these changes as each healed human on this Planet makes the world more healed.

Despite my pain, I regard every emotion and experience as a valuable lesson that shapes my identity. Our lives are precious gifts, and I strive to embrace this perspective with gratitude and hope the same for you.

What Did Gina Heal?

Gina Healed Myalgic Encephalomyelitis (ME)/Chronic Fatigue Syndrome (CFS)

I have experienced two seemingly insurmountable health challenges in my life. The first was Myalgic Encephalomyelitis/ Chronic Fatigue Syndrome (ME/CFS), as confirmed by my primary physician of now 37 years, Dr. Donald Plance. It was a debilitating condition, but with homeopathic remedies, mainly from Plance (i.e. L-Lysine, www.herbdoc.com detox, Lydia Pinkham herbal supplements, garlic, ginger, lemon, and organic foods, hot yoga, no dairy, no meat, and antiviral medications), meditations, and energy work, I was able to form natural antibodies and strengthen my immune system to overcome it and let my body calm from the meditation to stop the resistance of healing. This transformation has left me rarely getting sick and has given me what feels like a super immune system. The illness comes, and I can feel my body kicking into gear and performing as our incredible bodies were meant to. All along, I was doing the energy work to keep my physical essence in the highest forms of positive vibration possible.

The second affliction I faced was consistent suicidal ideation. I underwent a profound healing journey that not only cured me of this persistent struggle but also resulted in a significant spiritual and physical transformation. I believe that working with my spirituality was crucial in healing my soul and allowing my physical body to manifest the life I was meant to live.

Having experienced these challenges, I've come to realize that many individuals who are sensitive to energy face similar health issues, including ME/CFS. This is part of our journey to understanding our physical bodies and our connection to energy. Despite being considered incurable, I'm grateful to have found healing and wish to share my story with others, particularly those who may be facing similar health battles. I have connected with various groups to share my experiences and offer hope to those still struggling.

I firmly believe that spirituality plays a vital role in our overall well-being, and it's disheartening that it's often overlooked or approached as a last resort. I hope more people will prioritize their spiritual development as a fundamental part of their healing journey. I'm passionate about sharing this message, and I'm grateful to have this opportunity to connect with others who may be seeking a holistic approach to their well-being.

Do you want to be more youthful again? Work your energy!

Do you want to heal your mind and body? Work your energy!

Do you want to be connected to your life purpose? Work your energy!

Do you want to feel the love radiate through your being? Work your energy!

Do you want to set free the traumas and wounds you feel? Work your energy!

Do you want to transcend and connect with something that feels like a higher vibration? Work your energy!

Do you want to make Planet Earth a kinder place for all? Work your energy!

Do you want to call in the life you prefer to live with the people you like to surround yourself with? Work your energy!

Gina Healed Her Suicidal Ideation

Please know this: Just because suicide can feel like an energy of darkness, it doesn't mean anyone who does this will end up in the darkness; this is a myth. However, they can get stuck on

Planet Earth with their conscious confusion in transit, which will be explained more in future chapters. There is a way we can help them move on, too; often, it's us who are keeping them here because of our deep grief. Helping a soul onto their next lesson in love is one of the most generous things you can do. Their soul will always go home to all-encompassing love, and they will still be able to come back and check in with their loved ones. I have been guided in this book by some who have passed through suicide, and they are here supporting this expression. These souls want to offer help; it makes them feel good to contribute to our healing, so I listed and transcribed as best as possible.

Navigating the overwhelming experience of suicidal ideation can feel like an ongoing internal turmoil, with conflicting emotions and thoughts vying for control. At times, a glimmer of hope and positivity may emerge, only to be swiftly overshadowed by deep despair and an overwhelming desire to withdraw from everything and everyone. Because I had this show up in my life mainly during the worst of times, say a divorce or a job loss, I always knew it was hanging around in the background, waiting to come to the front at a moment's notice. I cannot tell you how relieved I am that I have healed this in myself to the point where if I even try to think about this level of cruelty to myself, I start to giggle, and my mind says to myself, "That is not you anymore." That is why I am here. I want to shout it to the rooftops to anyone who hears it. "You don't have to live the rest of your life with suicidal ideation. I am proof that it can be healed."

In my collaborative work with Dr. Amelia Kelley on the book titled *Surviving Suicidal Ideation: From Therapy to Spirituality and the Lived Experience* (published by the Swedenborg Foundation 2024), I chronicle my journey and the spiritual and energy practices that played a pivotal role in my recovery. Dr. Kelley provides invaluable clinical insights, offering understanding and support to individuals grappling with similar challenges. Within the book, I delve into the struggles I faced, which began with suicidal ideation at the tender age of eight. I also share anecdotal stories to provide context, offering a glimpse into the reasons behind the development of these ideas.

There are myriad reasons why one may experience suicidal thoughts, and I intimately comprehend the profound depths of this experience. I empathize with the agony and feeling trapped in what can seem like an impossible situation. Yet, here I stand, fortified and resolute, declaring that I have overcome and healed from the grip of suicidal thoughts and creativity. Even the most traumatic moments and periods of despair now feel like distant recollections, belonging to a time and person far removed from who I am now. If I can recondition and reshape my mind, body, spirit, and soul, utterly unaided by medication, then I am optimistic that many others can do the same. I aim to instill hope in those in need and convey that healing is possible. The most effective means of providing support is furnishing you with the tools outlined in this 6-week program, carefully tailored based on the proven methodologies harnessed at The Liberated Healer. While I lack formal training or certification to diagnose or treat this condition medically, I am compelled to share what has proven effective in my journey, hoping to offer aid to those who require it now if this book — *Planet Walking, A Handbook for the Living: A 6-Week Healing Program for Liberation and Specific Guidance on Suicidal Ideation*.

Suicidal Ideation, in terms of Spirituality, in some cases, is the death of a persona or an identity that needs to fall away, not the actual physical body that needs to die.

If and when you decide to undergo personal growth and transformation in this lifetime, you will experience a continuous process of change, much like the metamorphosis of a butterfly. This process involves shedding old aspects of your identity, which can be painful and bring about fears. Some people call this experience "ego death," but it's about letting go of parts of yourself that no longer serve you. It can be complicated to go through this process. For example, when I was married and deeply in love with my husband, I was devastated when he revealed that he was having an affair and wanted a divorce. I felt like my identity as his wife was crumbling, and I resisted letting go of it. The pain was so great that I wanted the suffering to go away, and I would obsess about killing the pain, which led to me thinking about suicide. However, it was that identity that was dying. If I knew then what I know now, I would honor that identity or part of me and more graciously let it go without the thought of something as devastating as removing me from this Planet. If I had not transitioned out of that relationship, I probably would never have found my soul's true mission and life, the life I have now, more aligned with who I am in my heart.

The Guides Explain the Above Concept Further

The idea that your soul is here at this time and place was a grand feat for you to get here! You planned to be here and deserve this life; no matter your story, you have a definite life purpose, and we will help you find that by the end of this book. The first purpose is to survive, which means ALL LIFE, including land, air, or sea creatures, plants, trees, bacteria, and beyond. We should be wanting to survive, but over the last few hundred years, a mental trend has been taking over, and that is suicide. We want to dispel what is happening with Spirituality so you can see it from a grander perspective.

Humans are ultimately looking at a permanent solution for a temporary problem. The desire for the death of the self ultimately comes from a person holding on to an IDENTITY that is not natural to them. They look at themselves and the world in a way that does not represent the true greatness within and around them. So, instead, this lens through which they perceive reality creates the experience of an inner and outer hell. So, the death that is desired is the death of the identity attached to the suffering they are experiencing. That is the desired transcendence; it is not the actual death of the body; that is not what they seek. In their desire for suicide, they are fundamentality desiring transcendence; they have not been given the tools for the condition, until now in this book, that allows for that transcendence to take place, so they tend to go into despair and hopelessness. These are WHY these sensations come up. The tools for transcendence and the knowledge for such are usually quite limited unless taught by someone who has mastered these skills (and why Gina has been tasked with creating these tools), and the person has become overly attached to a persona and an identity that is not healthy for them and does not represent them. Suppose they learn how to release that persona. In that case, if they know how to let the attachment to that identity go while being given the tools to discover the self that they genuinely are fundamentality, they can create that transcended experience they seek. There is always light in that darkness for people who are suffering from these types of suicidal ideations and urges. It is simply a matter of remaining dedicated to that light, even when the darkness seems to be most of what is perceived.

For example, as a child, Gina was driven to learn deeply about Spirituality. Still, her environment, friends, and places of work were no places where she felt comfortable talking about these subjects, so she pushed this desire down and would find subtle ways to learn and engage in this exploration. The exploration of Spirit was where her life purpose was hiding, but it would remain hidden until she dedicated herself to transforming. She would be suffering, not answering her calling. The good thing is that the Spirit is patient, always holds her, and gives her subtle signs to help guide her to where she needs to be.

Jules Verne 1828–1905, my first channeled piece of artwork 2008.

Symbolism in Spirit (an example)

The moon's cycles have always captivated humans, symbolizing our energy and continual evolution. It serves as a visual representation of our life cycle, reminding us of our interconnectedness. Looking back at a piece of artwork I created in 2024, I now understand its profound significance. At the time, I was grappling with intense feelings of despair and a strong desire to escape this world. I felt utterly lost and disconnected, believing I didn't belong and would never achieve my aspirations. Despite my unfamiliarity with Jules Verne, the renowned author, I was astonished to discover the connection between his work and my creation. It's only now that I recognize this piece's genuine nature and brilliance. It is a powerful testament to the transformative and healing impact of connecting with one's soul.

Here is what the image says to me after I have reached a more healed state.

- **Elements:** All four elements are represented: Earth, Fire, Wind, and Water.
- **Jules Verne**: A dreamer is just as valuable as an engineer if they do it with a heart-and-spirit connection. Follow Jules's path, and you will build worlds that inspire others and help them dream of healing. He is encapsulated in a giant pineapple as he carries all that it represents within.
- **Pineapple:** Life is a little bit sweet, prickly, and sour, but when you get to the core, it's neither; it is solid, who we all are at our core.
- **Moon:** The moon will follow you for your entire life here on Planet Earth, all while changing from light to shadow to darkness — but it always starts again. Like you will, but each time, you will have transformed just a little bit into a new, shinier version of yourself. There is always a part of you left in the dark; do not fear. This is the natural way of life. This is where the most reflection and lessons are learned — in the dark.
- **Volcano:** Don't fear the fire and the conflict, as a new seed is always birthed once the Earth has been scorched.
- **Time Piece:** Time is a function that connects us to the energy of the moon and gets us to the place we intend to go, but the best use of time is to be present in the here and now.
- **Light Code:** On the left side of Jules, tiny hearts are universal Light Codes of Love on repeat from a lost written language from early human life.
- **Squid:** The squid represents transformation. It changes its shape and appearance to adapt to its environment, perfectly representing those transforming their lives. It also represents intelligence and creativity, as it is

one of the most intelligent creatures in the ocean. They can communicate with others using a system of light and color changes, which is why it is often seen as a symbol of communication. They can represent the soul being transformed into universal collective energy — enlightenment. It's a symbol of water that helps to clean and purify.

Light (White, Colors, and Gold), Shadow (Greys), and Dark (Black) Energy

The light, shadow, and dark energy work together like a well-orchestrated dance; each needs the other to exist and can never be fully separated. I bring this up-front in education because when I first started, I wanted to clean myself from all darkness until I realized that it couldn't (shouldn't) be removed. I was missing the point: learning to coexist and hold the energy I preferred as much and as often as I chose. Without genuinely knowing how the dark and shadow energy feels, how can I learn, know, and understand how glorious the light feels?

Light and Dark Energy are based on the understanding that these two opposing forces are constantly intertwined in the realm of Spirit. Light and dark energies coexist, each taking turns to dominate or influence the other. It's essential to recognize that they are interdependent and cannot exist in isolation. Exploring the dynamics of working with light and dark energy is crucial for understanding their impact. For instance, when we find ourselves immersed in darker energy, such as during times of addiction or when surrounded by low vibrations, it can create vulnerabilities in our aura, allowing external energies to infiltrate. Engaging in practices that address these energies can help purify and strengthen the aura, providing protection, especially for those who resonate with this experience. Forms can be created like the visual of a dragon in your mind, but they are projections of the actual energy and can be used in the light, shadow, and dark imagery displaced to us. They are like a hologram where you could put your hand right through them. You have the natural strength with the body as we are here physically.

How to Use This Book

This text is a guide meant to accompany you on your journey, inviting you to write, make notes, and decorate its pages with coffee and tea stains and little sketches of your creative energy flowing out from your mind through your fingertips. You should be able to easily roll it up and tuck it away in your backpack, ready to share notes with others you encounter along your path of exploration. This concise program is designed to assist those seeking healing, drawing on my 15 years of research and practical experience. While a year may seem lengthy, it is a mere fraction of your lifelong quest. As you progress, you will undergo significant changes and experience a profound transformation; this cannot be rushed through a brief weekend course. It requires dedication, rituals, and time set aside to achieve this important objective, but the outcome will be a refined version of yourself equipped with the tools to navigate life's challenges and conflicts. Yet, it is essential also to appreciate and embrace the present moment and the opportunities that life presents to you.

These practices can be seamlessly integrated into any other program you are engaged in, whether religious teachings or therapy. They complement rather than hinder each other. These empowering tools are available 24/7, allowing you to utilize them anywhere, at any time, whether in a group setting or alone, through spoken words or silent reflection. These teachings form the foundational principles of The Liberated Healer™.

First Four Weeks: Foundational Learning

- You will feel significant shifts in this phase and be more grounded with a sense that you are taking your life into your own hands and managing your healing. You will gain more confidence to make these changes that once seemed impossible.

Last Two Weeks: Advanced Learning, Maintenance

- This phase will solidify your re-education, and as you evolve significantly, you will grasp more master principles and lessons.

The book covers many subjects that have inspired the creation of numerous books, videos, and other content. Due to the vastness of these subjects, it is not feasible to explain every aspect in-depth. Instead, the book presents many ideas and concepts with brief explanations to lay a solid foundation for understanding. In the "Resources" section at the back of the book, you will find recommended reading materials and experts in these categories. These resources will guide you to explore the subjects that interest you the most.

Please do your best to do other healthy activities as we process all of these activities and learnings like walking, earthing, going in nature, warm baths, strength, exercising where you can, and eating good food with vitamins, lots of water, and juices if you can with much appreciation for all those around you and who have provided you with yummy foods like the farmers and persons who help us enjoy this planet.

Does the Law of Attraction work? The answer is yes!

The law of attraction works because you are part of the universal energy. Your essence is part of the ecosystem, and you can connect to that energy at any time, and it can connect to you. Anytime you think your consciousness connects to the matrix. You bring about what you think about.

The Age of Aquarius Is Here for the Next 19 years – Huge Shifts

The universe, the Planet, its aura, and its inhabitants have patiently waited and held loving space for humans to make collectively positive changes. With authentic light worker groups gaining the strength to reveal the original codes and original messages edited to fit a few, we are being brought to the forefront of humanity to help. This is why truths about persons who put their interests before the public are appearing in the media. Planet Earth reacts to this energy in various ways, including the weather, because it radiates the energy we give it in war, celebrity worship, and how we are hurting the children, animals, and the elderly. Although parts will seem scary or even cruel, we are getting blessed with help to shift our consciousness to a higher vibration where we bring back our tribes, giving credit to where it deserves to persons in service like our teachers, scholars, farmers, and healers. The veil is being ripped off, and each person's healing matters, and we can get to the utopia of forgiveness as a collective once again.

Animals by Land, Sea, or Sky

These are sentient beings, and they are pure spirits. They can see dimensions that we cannot; they are only love. They should be cared for in the best possible way.

Plants, Trees, Bushes, Leaves, Roots, and Earth

These are sentient beings, and they are pure spirits. They can see dimensions that we cannot; they are only love. They should be cared for in the best possible way.

The Elements: Earth, Water, Air, and Fire

These elements are a part of us. Realizing your spiritual connection to them is true magic, and enlightenment will come over you. Learn how to work with and respect each element intentionally.

The Written and Expressed Voice(s)

I have discovered that my life purpose and gift is to be a cipher, and I learned this through the practices described in these pages on finding one's gifts and themes. As I write, some content comes from me, while some are guided to me by ascended masters, guides, and even angels. These books are created in spirit before being expressed in the physical world. This partnership is enriching, but at times, it can also be exhausting, especially when I feel the urgency to get everything I am seeing and hearing on paper so quickly that I worry the keyboard might burst into flames! I also receive great healing from this effort and am rewarded in many ways. I will share more details on how this process works in future lessons. Another concept that may seem magical and confusing is that you, the reader, are also a part of the creation of this book. Your search for something and your wants, needs, and desires have all contributed to forming the ideas and concepts within these pages. You are woven into the very fabric of this book. This realization serves as a reminder of our deep connections; thank you for your energy, trust, and understanding.

Updated Material

The subject matter is quite complex and constantly evolving. As we write this text, better ways may exist to explain the concepts, and future editions must be updated.

Artwork to Demonstrate Healing

Energy is neither created nor destroyed. It is just there as-is, waiting for you to use it or transform it like putty in your next creation.

The artwork is a collaborative effort between Gina and various guides to convey emotions, movement, and the workings of energy. The art contains therapeutic vibrations transmitted to viewers upon gazing at them. This is crucial because visual aids can help people learn more effectively, especially when they feel low or depressed and find it challenging to engage with written material. During my lowest moments, I found solace in absorbing the energies depicted in pictures and art, as my mind and heart were too burdened with engaging with lengthy instructions. Drawing from this experience, the guides and I collectively decided that this book could be a source of assistance for those in similar situations. The unique aspect of this expression lies in the fact that both the words and art originate from one source yet are influenced by many different souls. We will delve deeper into this as we progress further into the book.

Life is full of challenges, but you can overcome anything with the right tools. It may be necessary to learn how to navigate these challenges without letting them lead you into feelings of sadness, despair, or self-harm. It's okay – there is no judgment here. We can help you develop the skills to overcome these obstacles, and once you do, along with cultivating a deep love for yourself, you won't even consider harming yourself.

Knowing you are loved regardless of your past actions or experiences is essential. We are here to help you heal from any difficulties so that you and the world shine brighter.

We offer hope and guidance without promoting pharmaceuticals; all our recommendations are homeopathic. We also advise against self-diagnosis and encourage seeking professional therapeutic help when needed.

Religious Integration

The content of this book is not focused on any specific religion. It's recommended to consult with experts in religious studies for in-depth discussions on that topic. This program is designed to be adaptable to any belief system or spiritual orientation.

If your belief system has strict rules, you may experience strong resistance while reading this content. This resistance may manifest as intense sensations in your mind and body. If you encounter these feelings, reflecting on other areas of your life where similar resistance is present is essential. For instance, you might feel stagnant in your career or relationships and need more passion for the future. Our inner self signals that there's more to experience and that we are meant to learn and grow. Ignoring this inner guidance can create a self-imposed barrier preventing us from fulfilling our soul's purpose, potentially leading to mental and physical health issues. The lesson here is to understand how religion operates in our modern lives, with updated principles to live by, acknowledging that the world and our understanding of it have evolved.

The various names given to the divine – such as God, Source, Supreme Being, and others – are not separate from us but integral parts of our existence. It's a misconception that we are disconnected from God or Source. When we defer to a higher power by saying, "I'll leave it in the hands of ___," we essentially remove ourselves from the equation. In contrast, we should be actively engaged in personal transformation. We should take charge of making these transformations happen and trust that we have universal support beyond our imagination.

We have all heard about people using and abusing religions to gain control over people. To deny this in total would mean a complete unconscious expression. However there are good parts of these religions, but there is still energy programming to control and gain power over individuals. Each person needs to see their path, so you shouldn't take it upon yourself to try and steer another into anything else. Their path and soul will direct them. You can pray for people, put energy around them, and protect yourself, but jumping into their path is unhealthy for anyone. They have a spiritual contract that will be detailed in later pages. If you want to be deprogrammed, use the violet light we discuss in future dialogues. The ascended masters like Jesus, Mother Mary, Muhammad, Buddha, and more are real; call them in or any other angel or guide if you need help; they are always with you, and when you ask for a blessing or healing, you will receive it. When fear comes in about leaving a group or a practice, continue this work, which will help. Fear is no good in any context, especially in spirituality. But you should ask if it is a truth or a belief.

Expectations – 15 Years' Work Combined in 6 Weeks

We hope you feel deeply connected with yourself and the world as you read this book. Our goal is for you to realize how valuable your soul is and to feel more connected to everything and everyone. We want you to be inspired by the positive forces working to help you succeed with love, compassion, and empathy.

My healing journey took over 15 years, and it wasn't until a few years ago that I experienced a significant transformation. I want to help others achieve their transformations more quickly and effectively. Time seems to be moving faster, and we need to come together to raise each other's energy levels, embrace more love and empathy, and let go of judgment and shame.

If you open your heart to the teachings in this book and practice the energy and meditation techniques daily, even just for a few minutes, you will notice a shift in your energy. You might experience subtle changes or even profound physical and emotional transformations. As you let go of old belief systems and negative energies, a new version of yourself will emerge. It might initially feel unfamiliar, but you will start to see the world in a new light. You might even have experiences where you feel connected to other souls, the Earth, or the universe itself. As you progress through this journey, you will learn to judge others less, appreciate the beauty of life, and perhaps discover a passion or purpose that has been hidden within you. This program is part of The Liberated Healer's platform, designed to support you in your personal growth and healing.

Exercises:

What simplified vision would I like to see accomplished in this work for myself?

____

____

Giving Yourself a Permission Slip — Note to Self, Friends, and Family (if needed)

Permission slips are helpful when making significant changes because you need to confidently tell yourself that you are making this choice toward healing and that you permit yourself to make those changes. We have been programmed away from our calling in one way or another through the new societal norms. This "permission slip" will enable the process to begin. It's accepting the role it has in your life and allowing your energy to participate fully in the healing. Please be prepared when you feel comfortable with anyone helping you on your journey with this note. You can print it out and give it to them or post it, or you can say it to the universe, and they will still get your intended meaning.

Permission Slip

"I am a human becoming the soul I was meant to be, and I am starting a 90-day program to re-educate myself with my Spiritual birthright tools to assist me in growing and evolving. During this time, I might be sensitive or triggered as I look at myself, my relationships, and the energies I put into the world and attract while I study new ways to have a balanced and fulfilled life. I wanted you to know because you are essential to my life. Thank you for holding space for me as I dive into the unknown to rise within myself in seniority and sovereignty. I love you. Please forgive me. I am sorry. Thank you."

Dedication to Self-Contract

The following is a simple self-contract to dedicate this time to learning the tools to heal and liberate yourself. If this overwhelms you in the beginning, put it off to the side until you feel you can complete it without fear or anxiety. Don't push yourself when you are not ready. You are the only one who knows where you are always. Pay attention to those alarm bells. That is what we are working on, gentle, dear soul.

THIS IS ME, AND I AM HERE

Birth Name: ______________________________

Nicknames: ______________________________

Date/Place of My Birth: ______________________________

Relationships/Values: ______________________________

____

____

Things My Soul is Drawn to:

____

____

Features That Make Me Unique/Manifestations I am Interested in Bringing In:

____

____

____

Ideas, Habits, or Things I Want to Release:

____

____

I understand this is my journey and that I am unique and just as special as anyone else. As I uncover this uniqueness, I will realize how vital I am on this Planet now and that each of us has a purpose and role to be revealed over time. Some are revealed early on, and some may need to seek and search, but each path was just as it was written for me. May this new chapter benefit my awareness, understanding, and humor.

Date Signed: ____________ Signature: __________________________

It would be best to manage your emotions and triggers on this journey. We are here for you. We understand. This is not a judgment but support. If anything upsets you or you need more time to be ready to work that section, go to the next. This is natural and okay. Self-monitor to protect the most valuable thing in the world — you! Please reach out to us if you have any other questions at www.theliberatedhealer.com. *Please be kind and gentle with yourself on this journey.*

I Will Protect Myself, Slow, Gentle, Kind, Progress, and be Understanding.

I will know where I am emotionally and how I process this program and journey without self-judgment or criticism. I will only push myself into areas I am ready to engage with. I will reach out to get help when I need it from people in my life or the medical community as required.

Date Signed: ____________ Signature: __________________________

BUFFALO – Week 1 – The Liberated Healer's Foundational Teaching

The American Buffalo is our Spirit Animal for this week.

Being human can be challenging; it takes strength.
To do the work to heal from the inside out,
the buffalo has asked to be a part of this week's journey to
support anyone who needs that extra strength to get to
the other side of healing.

This powerful energy represents physical survival and Spiritual guidance,
with perseverance and the resilience to overcome obstacles.

Connecting All Things

A handbook for the living? Any correlation to the 1988 film *Beetlejuice* by Tim Burton, you say? Yes, of course, except for the obvious, this is a handbook for the living, not the deceased; thirty-five years ago, when this movie came out, I remember saying, "*What about a handbook for the living?* That is what I need!" As a child growing up in a chaotic and abusive household, these creative expressions via a film or a TV show lifted my Spirits and opened my eyes to worlds beyond my daily life. It is a vehicle for many worldwide to help dream of their potential future. These creative expressions are also curated from energy and Spirit, from the people who dream them into reality, from their energy, from the light and the dark. It is communication as humankind created storytelling, and it is powerful. It can transform us in many fascinating ways. It is why I was driven into the entertainment business; I envisioned a world where people were buzzing with stories and people came together to sing, dance, and laugh because they (to me) would have had the very best job in the world. But, when I got there, this was not my experience.

I kept trying to make it so, but the people I aligned with were filled with pain, regret, fear, and control. I kept trying to find the light in this space with new groups, but always met with the same energy. It latched onto my traumas and insecurities created in my childhood. It reflected the enhanced storylines I had made that I was unworthy, untalented, stupid, and unloved. I blamed the industry, but it was all I knew. I was offered three different roles at The Walt Disney Company at nineteen. From there, I went to Twentieth Century-Fox, Creative Agencies, and finally to Warner Bros., gaining my ultimate dream studio job.

I worked hard. I was your typical unhealed, traumatized, anxious worker who thought the more time I worked, the more effort I put in, the more likely I was to have the life I wanted. I was on the hamster wheel with hopes and dreams of getting off and enjoying the life I had built, surrounded by love and friends who passionately supported each other with kindness. But this was not the case; of course, there were glimpses of great things, but I couldn't get into the flow. These jobs are very polarizing and filled with unsurmountable pressure, and if you let them see your weak spots, they would go in for the jugular. You are on a constant trampoline of emotions, and I did find many like me who were also unhealed and traumatized people who were poking at each other's triggers repeatedly. I didn't know then what I know now, which is what this first week will be about, how much I needed to learn about my energy, and what I was putting into the world.

Our Energetic Being

This is a big topic, so we will focus on what you need to know to do this work; this topic will constantly evolve throughout the book with information that applies to the topic. The resources section will include detailed book recommendations if you want to learn more about this fascinating part of who you are. The energy centers we focus on are our chakras, which correspond to the other layers in the aura, and how those centers communicate with the circle of our being, including our Spirit. See the detailed artwork below as we refer to the areas of conversation.

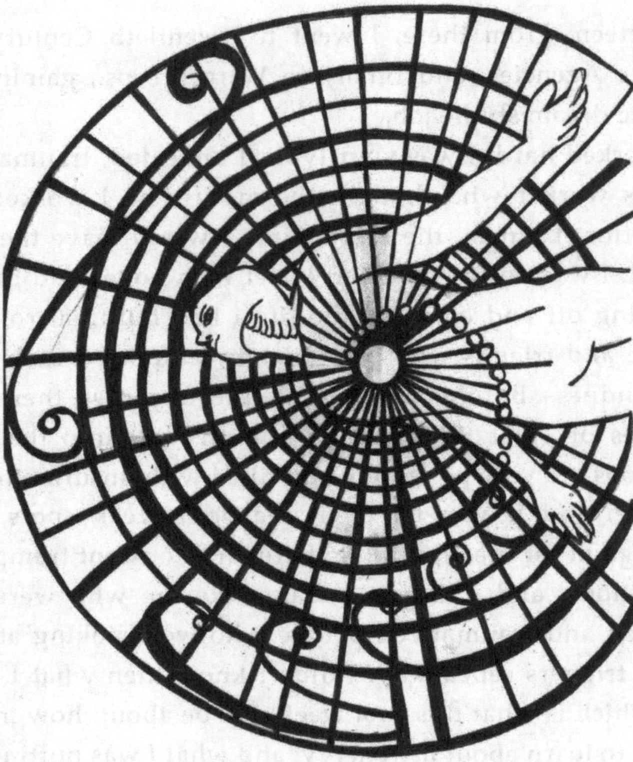

Your Aura and Energy System

Week 1. Day 1 – Invocation, Connecting All Things, What Is Energy, Protection Rose and Body of Glass

Practice: Protect Your Energy

What is energy? Within each of us resides an astonishing 50 trillion cells, each teeming with the vibrancy of electrons, protons, and atoms, generating a swirling, pulsating vortex of energy that envelops us. It's akin to the ripple effect caused by a stone dropped into a serene pond; our energy radiates outwards, affecting everything around us. Negative energies like hate, revenge, and fear disrupt this energy field, unleashing a powerful force that impacts our beings and those in our vicinity. Conversely, positive energies such as love, happiness, and joy can have a similarly potent influence. Picture a tornado with its whirlwind of energy capable of sweeping through and transforming anything in its path. We are like these energetic whirlwinds with the potential to shape our surroundings. We must learn to harness and direct our energy to wield its power wisely.

Going back, so we can go forward. Humans tend to focus too much on one side, but you must look at all sides to have a harmonious life. With these skills, you can get through many things that are hard about being human. Because of our modern age, we have lost our instincts about protecting our energies and abandoned spirituality as the primary tool. In the past, all humans knew about these fundamental understandings, and through time, they have been programmed out of us to control us. That is why, as we have become more modern and more prosperous as a society, we are sicker, on more medication, and struggling with a variety of mental, emotional, and physical health issues. This is where we are getting "social contagion." This work will help reset you, but you must practice. It's not a magic pill.

Please know that you have been brave and strong through all the things you have had to overcome. We are meant to build that strength through these learning opportunities. That each one makes you a warrior for yourself. Life is a flow, up and down, just like that river.

Timing. Take your time as you learn the practice; once you understand, you can perform most of these things in seconds.

Results. Please remember you can't do this wrong; learning the steps is necessary, but everyone has their cadence and the best way to receive information. The **intention** is the most essential part.

Intention. The intention is to protect your energy in your space and to keep others' low vibration out of your space. The more we run our energy, the more balanced we are, and the more we can work on transforming the things we are working on and manifesting the future we desire.

You will hear the word ENERGY so much that it will start to feel redundant. It is the best word to explain what we will transmit inside and out of you. So, hold it in high regard and become friends because we are about to go on an energy journey. That is why this book is an endeavor; this is not a weekend course for a reason. There is much to learn, but this work will integrate into your lives in ways that can change you for the rest of your time here on Earth. Some people are susceptible to others' energies, and they have a hard time separating their energy from others. What if you are carrying someone that you love, their energy is depressive, and you think it is yours? That happens; you want to help them so much your Spirit agrees to take it, but it hurts both of you. If you're going to help anyone else, you must start with — YOU.

Protection Rose, Body of Glass, and Protect Your Energy. *This is a 30 to 45-minute practice.*

1. When we ask the Spirit to create something or remove it, we are giving it a command, and it listens immediately and very well.
2. You can do this with your eyes open or closed. Initially, we suggest you close your eyes if it is safe.
3. You have a round, spherical energy around your physical body, which most people identify as your Aura. Image this body of energy around you; this is your space.
4. Imagine a large open rose with a stem and leaves just outside the aura. Give that rose an elongated cord coming off the stem and sending it to the Center of the Earth.

5. Tell your Spirit to use this rose to protect your energy.
6. Your energy will stay inside with you and be protected, and outside energy will remain beyond the rose, unable to penetrate your space.
7. This helps so you can work on your energy only and not that of other people. It also helps when pushing out potential dark energies in your space because this is a loving gesture to yourself and raises your frequency.
8. Don't worry; this does not mean the people you love or want to be around will be moved out of your space. This sets an energetic boundary so you can work your energy with intention.
9. You now have your "Protection Rose." Please do this before we start any energy work or throughout the day, before bed, driving, work, or a meeting!
10. **BODY OF GLASS** – Extra protection if needed: Some people are sensitive and might have psychic attacks from other energies. If you feel this might be you, add this extra step of protection. Image your entire body is GLASS. This will create a non-sticky energy around you, so if anyone throws it at you, it will just slide off! Go to Grounding Cord next to do this so it falls away appropriately. This is a neutral space for all energy.

Week 1. Day 2 – Teaching: Like Energy Attracts Like Energy

They Mirrored Souls/Relationships. The bond between individuals is often based on a shared energy. When one person goes through significant changes while the other remains stagnant, the harmony in the relationship is disrupted. This shift is an important reason why more than half of marriages end in divorce. It's not a judgment but an acknowledgment of everyone's unique journey. Some people prefer gradual personal growth, opting for a slower, more relaxed pace in life.

However, life has a way of nudging them towards change and development, aligning with their destiny.

Later lessons will delve deeper into these concepts and their connection to soul contracts and destiny. For instance, sustaining a relationship requires an intentional effort from both parties to evolve together in all aspects of life. It demands work and dedication but signifies the mutual decision to embark on this transformative journey with a chosen partner. Energetically, it becomes apparent when the relationship no longer nurtures growth, passion, creativity, expression, and spirituality. This may indicate that the soul contract with this individual has run its course, and both individuals are meant to pursue new experiences. Letting go can be challenging, but doing so with kindness may be the most compassionate gesture for both parties, allowing each soul to explore new avenues of growth.

Learning about these concepts has relieved the pressure for me, as I've come to understand that it's okay to acknowledge when two individuals have grown apart. It doesn't necessarily result in a negative or hurtful outcome but signifies a natural evolution. Releasing someone with love means acknowledging the love shared will endure, transforming into a different relationship. Our closest connections often serve as mirrors, reflecting aspects of ourselves. When two individuals veer off in different directions, they no longer converge at the midpoint, where their mirrored reflections also converge. This natural distancing is the universe's way of signaling that learning and growth with that soul has reached its culmination. This realization doesn't diminish the love that existed; rather, it signifies that an abundance of love has fostered the decision for both souls to embark on new journeys out of love and respect for each other.

My Example: I used to be a troubled and imaginative individual carrying unresolved emotional pain and harboring negative beliefs about myself. I was drawn to similar people because we shared the same inner turmoil, allowing us to relate. The problem was that I would consistently try to support and uplift them, believing they deserved love, but I should have extended that same care and compassion to myself. This pattern drained me, and I was eventually trapped in unfulfilling relationships with blurred boundaries. We were all wounded and struggling, perpetuating a cycle of tension and toxic interactions. Recognizing this, I have been dedicated to transforming these patterns within myself, and I'm grateful to say that I have seen positive changes.

The New Me: I have transformed myself to become healthier, more grounded, and more balanced, which has led me to attract a higher quality of people, projects, and relationships. My elevated frequency has brought individuals into my life who resonate with my energy, allowing for meaningful connections and understanding.

I've also discovered I can still thrive in the entertainment industry, surrounded by wonderful people and engaging projects. I struggled with challenging situations and roles because I needed to focus on my personal growth. During times of self-doubt and feeling disconnected, I would question why I was putting in so much effort every day yet still feeling unfulfilled. It became clear that I wasn't living my life's purpose, and at one point, I wasn't even sure what that purpose was. This left me feeling lost and unsure if I would ever find my true calling, making me feel like I was wasting my time somehow. This led to a cycle of declining health, attracting more drama and unintentionally causing pain to those around me.

I sought validation by trying to heal others to make myself feel more valuable. However, I would become resentful when my efforts weren't appreciated. I also allowed people who didn't deserve my time or energy into my life because I believed that was all I deserved. Even though I knew the kind of relationships I truly desired, I settled for less because I felt it was all I could attain (or so I believed).

You must, must, must use that energy to heal yourself. When you are healed or just beginning to move in that direction — what is truly meant for you will start to show up for you. It will show up, and you will recognize it as your intuition sharpens. That has changed now; I have a solid and unique circle of people in my life. Each of them brings a different quality to the table. Still, we all have the baseline that I demand to engage in kindness, thoughtful interactions, intelligent communication, fun and laughter, and mutually balanced support.

We are starting with this to set up the first few days with intentions. It is to recognize your energy, what you call in, and what you are vibrating into the world. The following days will set you up for your meditations to do all this work.

Energy Review

Once you are trained in Rosework, which will be a few days from now, we will return to these questions and answers for practice.

What energy do you think you give off to others versus what energy do you think you are hiding inside that we need to work on? *Example: "I give off the energy of confidence and expertise, but inside, I feel left out, alone, and judged."*

____

____

____

What themes or patterns in your life do you recognize as unhealthy but are such a part of you that you fear letting them go? *Example: "I fear setting strict boundaries with others as they might leave me. I recognize that others and I rely too much on substances like alcohol in our relationships, but it makes me feel more connected and open, and I am afraid not to have it in my life."*

Looking in "general" at the people, projects, and things you created in your life, what are some of the repeat energies/themes you can see that you keep calling in? *Example: "I seem to call in people who are not available emotionally or have addiction issues. I feel used to my energy and resources when they leave and that the relationships are not balanced, but I am fearful of letting them go as I have abandonment wounds."*

Are you considerate of those around you? Are the people around you considerate of you?

Are you trusting with strangers? Do you think strangers are trusting of you?

Do you enjoy sharing with others? Do you think others enjoy sharing with you?

Do you make cultivating your relationships a high priority? Do the people around you develop relationships, too?

Are you generous? Are the people around you generous?

Do you frequently feel gratitude and count your blessings? Do the people around you feel gratitude back?

Do you love most people (by your definition)? Do the people around you love most people back?

Are you easily able to extend compassion to others and yourself?

Do you make a daily effort to make the people around you feel better? Do the people around you make a daily effort to make you feel good?

Do you or would you hug, hold, or cuddle something else if you could daily?

Do you feel elated when something good happens to someone else? Do the people around you feel elated when something good happens to you?

Great job! Thank you for being open and honest with yourself. Again, we will leave these answers here for the next few days when you learn "Rosework" so we can use them as starter questions for you to practice. First, we need a few more tools. You will learn how to set yourself up to receive and transform your gathering knowledge!

Week 1. Day 3 – Meditation 1, Grounding and Releasing, Setting Up Your Space

This day, we will apply your protection rose or body of glass (or both) and ground yourself and your space or location. This is a 30 to 45-minute practice.

Grounding is your new best friend. I ground when I feel a tense event, conflict, trigger, or something that makes me anxious. It is the number one tool used for many things regarding energy work. It puts your power into your own hands so you can take the driver's seat in anything in life. When you get used to this practice, you will wonder how life existed without it. You will also clearly see why you were struggling. We mentioned earlier that about 200 years ago, humankind started having mental struggles and suicidal ideation when previously persons were driven to live. Through the introduction of big money (the steam trains and coal) and modern living, we lost the tribal Spirit over time. It's part of why kids are feeling so disconnected. They were meant to play in trees and fish in streams, not do quirky dances for likes. This is the way of the new world, so we must all learn how to reconnect, and grounding will do this.

You can ground anything, and we will do so together. Ground yourself, ground your room, your office, your car, your block, animals, projects, relationships, friends, strangers, large parts of the Planet, the ocean, any object ... anything you want to be grounded in more reality and present time.

Ground your animals. I have rescue animals, and my one smaller dog was extremely abused and lived in the hot and cold elements until I got him. He shakes all the time in terror. If this is your animal or even if they are not traumatized, see if you can feel their subtle shifts while grounding. They love healing! Feel their energy with your hands and close your eyes. You should feel a buzzing in your hand. Please give them a grounding cord and send it to the center of the Earth. I can always feel my sweet dog's buzzing start to subside.

Morning Grounding. I wake up with anxiety from my past traumas, still to this day, on most days. I don't beat myself up about it; it's a part of me. I turn my tools on, and it sets my day up for success, healing, and kindness for myself – activating self-love. I do this just as I open my eyes, and then I get up and do it more formally after I've done my morning routine, but this takes the buzzing out of my space and gets me ready to tackle anything throughout the day.

> *If you wake up with anxiety – it's because you are thinking about the past or the future when you go to bed, and it is carrying over to the morning.*

Here are the steps we will be mastering. The drawing is a little challenging to understand (an animation would have been great), but this image will be more transparent once you learn it.

1. *Grounding*
2. *Earth*
3. *Cosmic*
4. *Combine Earth 10% & Cosmic 90%*
5. *Bring up the Front Half of your body through the Crown Chakra (like a fountain out of the head) and cover your auric bubble*
6. *Protection Rose/Body of Glass*
7. *Golden Suns to recall your life force energy*

Running and Cleaning Your Energy Diagram

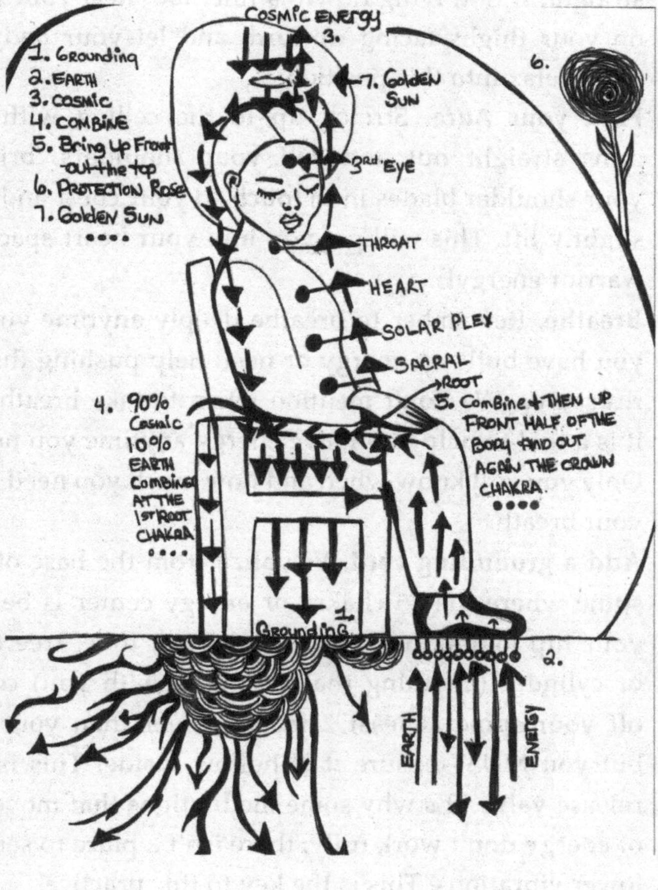

Meditation 1 Process: You can and should practice grounding anything and everything. Know why you do this and don't and how the energy feels different.

- **Take the corners of your mouth and point them up.** Remember to have FUN if you can! The best way to break up energy is laughter and a smile; this shouldn't be too serious. If you can't do it right now, we can still pretend to laugh, which helps with a gentle "ha, ha, ha, ha."
- **Assume position.** Close your eyes. If you can, sit in a chair with your feet on the ground and your back very straight; if not, lying down is fine, too. Rest your palms on your thighs facing upward, and let your body and mind relax into this position.
- **Find your Aura.** Stretch up to the ceiling with your arms straight out and roll your shoulders, bringing your shoulder blades in to touch so your chest and heart slightly lift. This will get you into your heart space and warrior energy!
- **Breathe.** Remember to breathe deeply anytime you feel you have built-up energy or need help pushing through resistance. We don't mention when to take breaths, but it is a tool to help you move energy anytime you need it. Only you will know when and how much you need to use your breath.
- **Add a grounding cord.** Visualize from the base of your spine where the 1st chakra or energy center is between your hip joints. Imagine a large cord, tube, tree trunk, or cylinder (anything that resonates with you) coming off your spine at least 2 inches wider than your hips, but you MUST ensure it is hollow inside. This is your release valve. It's why some meditations that move a lot of energy don't work fully; there isn't a place to send the lower vibrations. This is the key to this practice.

- **Center of the Earth.** I want you to visualize that cord hitting the ground and traveling like the speed of light to the center of the Earth, where the lava is, and connecting there. You can say out loud or to yourself, but again, the Spirit will do what you indicate, *"Please release any energy that is not mine, that is not serving me at this time, down the grounding cord to the center of the Earth, and let it burn away."*

Note: When a person is grounded, it is much harder to shake that person physically, emotionally, or mentally. This is why this is great for leaders with a lot of stress. This cord will also help with your seniority in any situation and help build confidence.

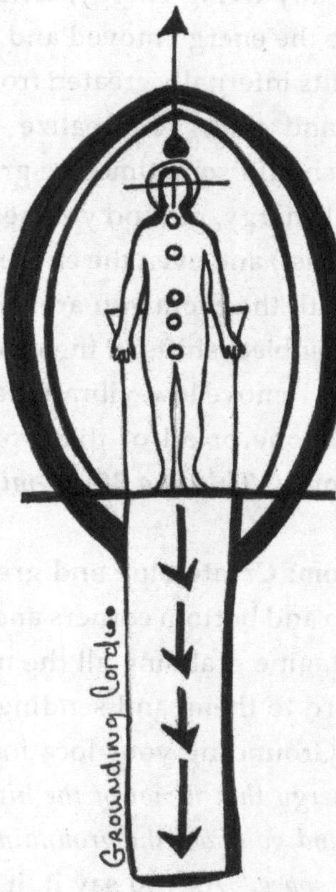

The Grounding Cord and Aura Bubble

TIP: If you resonate with sounds and music and have anxiety or panic attack disorder, this will help! Get a speaker that can be voice-activated, such as Alexa or iHome. When you are in a low mood, the faster and easier you can access calming energy, the better. I use this through the night with "ocean sounds." Upon waking, I perform "meditation music" with a low hum throughout the day. It helps keep my emotions and energy on a positive frequency.

Grounding Cord, Aura, and Major Chakras

Grounding You, Locations, Animals, and Friends

Everything that has any living energy, whether it is around it or not, needs to have the energy moved and worked. Even your computer has elements internally created from organic material. When you understand that, you realize that anything and everything can and should sometimes be grounded. When you are doing intentional energy, ground yourself first, and then the room you are in (at least) and even the entire house, complex, or street. Please start with the room you are meditating in and try to keep aware of the subject shifts in the room.

The intention is to remove low-vibrational energy from your location. You can do one or all of these practices, whichever resonates with you most. ***This is a 30–45-minute practice.***

- **Owning a room:** Create blue and green neon lines from the room's top and bottom corners and have them meet in the center. Imagine grabbing all the neon lines, adding a grounding cord to them, and sending them to the center of the Earth. Grounding your location: Think or say out loud, *"Any energy that is not of the highest vibration, let it hit the lasers and go down the grounding cord, cleaning and protecting this space."* As you say it, it will happen as you are commanding it. This puts you in the power position.

- **Cleaning Out a Room:** Ground the room just like you did when grounding yourself by imagining a large grounding cord around the whole section. Imagine roses on each wall or even filling each room from the floor to the ceiling with as many roses as you can visualize. Low vibrations cannot live in this grounded energy with roses. Imagine a large golden sun over the entire location and say, "We recall all the original life force energy from this place to a neutral and high vibration."
- **Set the Energy of the Room:** Decide what vibration you would like in that room and what color represents that vibration (see color chart below). Give the room a color wash of that color from the floor to the ceiling, or place a big rose of that energy in the middle of the room. For example, as blue is an excellent color for communication, use bright blue for your office space to encourage and help ensure that the location is quickly moving through that blue energy so you can be seen and heard with clear communication channels. As mentioned above, ground the area and give it a Golden Sun to bring in fresh energy.

Week 1. Day 4 – Earth and Cosmic (Running Your Energy)

This day, we will apply your protection rose or body of glass (or both), ground yourself and your space or location and run your energy using the Earth and cosmic technique. This is a 30 to 45-minute practice.

- **Awaken:** Bend down in the chair and touch your toes. Wiggle your toes if you can while taking nose inhales (no mouth breathing, if possible). A quarter-sized chakra is in the center of your foot. Open and close it so you know where it is; leave it open.

- **Earth Energy:** Imagine getting a nice piece of Earth energy and bringing it into the open foot chakra. Let it travel up either in circles or straight up into the feet, the ankle, the calf, the knee, the thighs, and the base of your spine, where we rest on the 1st chakra (aka the Sacral Chakra).
- **Cosmic Energy:** About an inch above your head is the 7th chakra, which is flat like a little pancake. Open and close it so you know where it is; leave it open. Imagine going from where you are out of your body (your Spirit) and traveling above the Earth to the universe, where you feel the weightlessness of your Spirit. See, feel, and hear the Planets, the stars, the black holes, and travel to a star and reach out and grab some of that fluffy "stardust" energy as it turns into a bright rainbow of colors with the highest vibrations your mind can imagine. Let that energy return to Earth and enter that 7th chakra you left open and go right into your spine, illuminating your entire body as it combines with the spinal fluid. This will align the back half of the body as we go down the 33 vertebrae and hit each one.
- **Earth & Cosmic Combine:** When it gets to the base of your spine, combine the two energies, 90% Cosmic and 10% Earth, and repeat this in your head or out loud a few times. Once combined, let that come up the front half of the body, aligning your entire energetic body and chakras — like magnets, they will all go into place. While doing that, they shift off low-vibrational energy down the grounding cord.
- **Fountain from the top of the head:** Let that combination shoot through the 7th chakra and form around the aura, giving you a mini cleaning. Now, let the energy go down your arms.
- **Fountain the energy out of the hand chakras:** Lay your hands on your thighs, facing the ceiling. The hand chakras

are the size of a quarter in the palms of your hands. Imagine them opening and closing, then leaving them open and letting this Earth and cosmic energy fountain out of the hands.

Celebrate! You are now running the complete energy system!

Week 1. Day 5 – Golden Sun, Present Time

This day, we will apply your protection rose or body of glass (or both), ground yourself and your space or location and run your energy using the Earth and cosmic technique. Recall your life force energy with Golden Suns and bring yourself into the present time. This is a 30 to 45-minute practice.

Golden Sun. It's time to fill back up all the good energy with Golden Suns and recall your life force energy. If you can look at yourself like a glass of energy and look at what is inside, what are you full of? Grounding is like a way to release the low-level energy that is not serving you or like taking the steam out of the tea kettle getting ready to explode. The Golden Sun brings back the high-level energy and fills you up.

- **Close or open your eyes in meditation:** Create a giant bubble just behind the back of your head, and let it grow and expand with gold/white light. Imagine it's like a big magnet calling your life force energy inside the bubble, where it can collect. It should feel warm, inviting, loving, calm, and full of life, like the natural sun on your face after the rains have parted.
- **Ask your Spirit:** *"Please bring back my original life force energy."* You can recall this energy from a specific person, job, situation, or anything else you can to take back your energy. You should do this for everyone, even those you love the most, so you can continue to give to them.

It doesn't hurt anyone but refills you, so you can give again, starting with the self.

This is a vital part of the process. Often, people forget to replenish their energy, and they feel depleted. Always remember that when you ground, you need clean, new energy.

Present-Time

We must be present in the day to make the changes we want to see in ourselves and the world. This is not easy as we are programmed at this time in humanity to live in the past patterns that our life has experienced and, in the future, as we hope and pray for the life we want to live. Both serve us in moving forward when we are healing, and this will be detailed later, but we must be present today to appreciate where we are, so we know where we want to go.

This can be very difficult, and I must share that it was tough for me and still can be sometimes. I tend to live in the future and dream of worlds and situations that are not what I am experiencing now. A little of that is needed to manifest the life you want, but there needs to be a balance, and when we meditate and work on ourselves, we must be here and in the now!

- You can do this in a variety of ways that speak to you.
  - You can imagine writing the date on your grounding cord and signing it with your signature.
  - You can tell the whole date to the universe three times, bringing you into the present.
  - In the next couple of sections, you can look at your rose and ask, "How much of my energy is in the present time?" You will usually get a number that is not 100%. We will work over this course to bring you into a higher present-time ratio.

Repeat and return to today when you feel yourself drifting off and away into the past or the future. This is where we can do the most work on healing.

Week 1. Day 6 – Center of Your Own Head, Tying It All Together

This day, we will apply your protection rose or body of glass (or both), ground yourself and your space or location, and run your energy using the Earth and cosmic technique.

Recall your life force energy with Golden Suns, bring yourself into the present time, and now you will learn how to be in the center of your head (pushing out other people's energies and thoughts). From this point forward, when you are asked to start the "Foundational Meditation for the Day," please start this complete process. This is a 30 to 45-minute practice.

A lot of the time, it's the mind that is the culprit with unbalanced behavior, uncontrollable thoughts, and negative thinking. Many of us know this to be accurate, but we will let other people, ideas, thoughts, emotions, and programming come into our space, and it conflicts with who and what we are at the core. How can we make the right decisions and trust our intuition if we have 100 people in there shouting at us? I have seen some people have that many people's energy inside of them. We can get this from people in our space and through media through overt and covert messages put out into the world.

You have tools now to reset this energy. This is the last part of the first week and is very important. It also takes practice because we are used to having all those people's energies and thoughts in our minds.

- Get through the Foundational Meditation above and try to locate the center of your head as you meditate. I recommend gently tapping your forehead several times to find the exact area. It calls your entire being to this location.
- Create an image of a miniature version of yourself sitting precisely as you are. You can almost copy yourself just as you are sitting in your chair, but make yourself only a few inches in size and place yourself in a chair inside the center of your head.
- Add a grounding cord to this smaller version of yourself, send that cord to the center of the Earth, and ask that you release any energy that is not yours out of the center of your head.
- Imagine you are surrounded by white light, and that light is growing in your head. As it is, it is also pushing all these other people's thoughts and energies out until you are sitting in a White Room all by yourself.
- Put a smile on your face and raise the corners of your mouth – you have achieved a significant milestone!

Week 1. Day 7 – Day of Rest, Integration

You've reached a significant milestone, and you should take a moment to acknowledge the hard work you've put in. You prioritized your well-being on this journey, and that's truly commendable. The best part is that you achieved healing and growth without relying on anyone else. You've acquired valuable tools, knowledge, and spiritual insights that will always be a part of you. These foundational resources will support you as you navigate through life's challenges.

Today, giving yourself the time to rest and allow your progress to become integrated into your being is essential. Pay attention to subtle changes and any emerging thoughts or emotions. Take a moment to reflect on the things on your mind and consider what aspects you would like to work on in the upcoming weeks. Did you experience vivid visions, see colors, or feel sensations in your body? It's common for us to seek external solutions or rely on medication to bring about balance. Still, it's essential to recognize the power of inner practices before turning to pharmaceutical intervention, especially for children who are still developing.

Write. Thank you for trusting in yourself and the process. Let the world fall in love with this new version of yourself as it manifests. Please attend calming events today or go to nature, the universe, the guides, and all the energy around you to celebrate this first week with you!

Draw. Let go of some of the energy that moved this week, an animal, tree, or a part of nature that you connected with physically or in the mind. When you apply ink to the paper, you realize the release and activation of new energies through teachers, friends, and lovers and open your intelligence to connect more with yourself and your guides.

Draw any image inside this circle. If you're unable to create a picture, outline the proposed drawing. Through this practice, you'll release any trapped energy via the ink as it flows out from you. Take note of your thoughts. If you encounter a negative self-directed thought, visualize discarding it through a grounding cord. You actively manage your self-talk each time you engage in this activity. This exercise is beneficial, especially for individuals who struggle with meditation. After a few minutes, attempt to meditate once more.

Spiritual Warrior You Are

ELEPHANT – Week 2 – As Above (Spirit), So Below (Physical)

You're a Sovereign Being (a Re-Education) – As Above (Spirit), So Below (Physical Body)

The Asian and African elephants are our
Spirit animals for this week.

They are the sheer power that underpins the Chakra system.

We want to bring a gentle cadence and compassion
for you and this beautiful Planet this week.

Earth has more unique species than any other Planet in the Universe.
That is special, and so are you. We need your voice
and love in this world. We will hold space for
you until you can hold it for yourself. We love you so much.
One day, when you are strong, you may find enough
energy to send it back to us as we fight for our existence
with love and gratitude.

Week 2. Day 1 – Your Soul Frequency

As above (Spirit), so below (body) meaning. I came across a saying that resonated with me and holds a lot of truth. It conveys that if your spirit is not well, it will reflect your physical health. Even when faced with physical illness, if your spirit is strong and in harmony, you can still find peace and contentment in your chosen life. Despite facing immense challenges and rare genetic diseases, I've been inspired by individuals who demonstrate incredible resilience and show us the true meaning of life. In a society where many are focused on external appearances, these individuals teach us about the immense strength of the human spirit. So, if we genuinely want to heal and take care of ourselves, we should understand our bodies and what works best for them, and in doing so, we can safeguard and nurture our spiritual well-being.

What does your soul look like, and what is its signature frequency?

Each of us carries a unique signature frequency of sound and vibration that is exclusively our own. This distinct frequency, which resonates with our essence, allows evolved souls to communicate, recognize, and understand one another. As we progress on our spiritual journey, we strive to align this frequency with the present moment, thereby facilitating positive transformations in our lives and making it easier to connect with soulmates, such as twin flames, and experience profound spiritual connections. Those vibrating at this distinct frequency do not identify others by their physical name but by their unique vibratory frequency.

There are ways to determine what would be considered a being's higher spiritual name when the soul was created. Wouldn't it be neat to know your original name? These techniques can be calculated through astrological charts but not through a usual reading. A chart reading must be explicitly done, where all the degrees of the Zodiacal wheel are converted into letters, and specific alignments are read. This produces a soul name that, when utilized, awakens the person's higher self. I am still seeking people who can do this, as it is a rare talent.

My Oversoul (pictured below). The Oversoul is the principal and primary soul encompassing a person's information. It's like the essence of who you are at the deepest level. Over time, this soul evolves and transforms, taking on new colors and imagery as it gains wisdom and accumulates more experiences, specifically those related to dharma and karma, detailed in future lessons.

The delicate lines within the Oversoul represent the different active lives that my soul is currently engaged in. There are 12 active lives, and if you consider the entire Oversoul, there are 13 lives. The circles on the outer ring symbolize all the complete past lives that I have lived. The feathering around the edges of the Oversoul moves with the winds of change, aiding in the flow of energy. The energy flows through the left and out through the right, pulsating the entire system. At the bottom is a thin line known as the "etheric cord," which connects to the physical body, ensuring I remain linked to all my active lives. Picture the soul vibrating and dancing, brimming with colors and resonating with sounds rippling through a vibrant frequency.

What Gina's Soul (kind of) looks like; the circles in the center represent her past lives:

What a client's soul (kind of) looks like; the circles in the antenna of the little creature on top represent their past lives:

Here are some highlights about your soul; please circle or note the things you want clarification on, and when you learn how to get your questions answered directly, you can practice with these questions.

- If you have a human body, you are stronger than you think, no matter where you are from, your life experience, or your abilities or disabilities. Any other outside energy, light or dark, cannot match what a soul can do in a physical body — the game changes once you learn that the power is all within you. Your Spirit is powerful and limitless; our hardwiring stops us, and that can be changed with practice and intention.
- Your soul is as unique as a fingerprint; every soul has a purpose to elevate humanity, the collective, and itself. Your unique journey has been designed to evolve your soul. You will most likely return if you gain karma (a thing that you have gone against another that has not been healed — see reincarnation in later sections).
- Your soul has a unique sound vibration that is only yours, and it is an original name that can be identified if you get to a specific level of ability in meditation or are a qualified astrologist.
- Every soul came from a "soul spark" from an all-encompassing light and love source.
- Every child with a soul comes in with ultimate empathy and compassion. The Earth plane and the dark energy here can turn people toward the dark. It is not their original intention, and we can heal this! This book includes all the tools you might need to rid yourself, your space, your projects, your families, and your homes of these darker energies (they are just energies and not as powerful as a human soul).

- Love, joy, laughter, and forgiveness are the highest vibrational energy.
- You always have guides with you. Everyone is born with at least two guides, one of whom is a guardian angel who stays with them until they leave their body. You are never alone.
- If you prioritize Spirituality like our ancestors, we will all become happier. We have been programmed to make this the last endeavor when we are miserable and desperate for healing. In these modern times, some people will try everything BUT Spirituality.
- You can call any ascended master, guide passed family member, or loved one living or passed to help you when needed, and they are there. Since they are just energy, they can be anywhere and everywhere, all at the same time.
- Meditation, Prayers, and Rituals work! Lean into love, and you will attract more love; lean into fear, and you will attract more fear.
- No matter your circumstances, it will be improved by deepening a spiritual practice.
- Every single person has an entire universe of opportunities in their hands.
- Every soul is one string on a tapestry that bends and moves as it ages. If you cut that string, it weakens the whole piece, and that is how vital you are. When you KNOW this, your life will change.
- The people you are angry with, hate, and distrust have all played this game with you before, and perhaps it was their turn to be the wrong person. We are all playing parts in our own very intense play.
- If you play it safe and make no effort to change or learn about yourself, others, and the world around you, you

are not cheating the game; you are cheating yourself. Everyone must do the work; nobody gets away without doing the work.

- As you connect more with your Spiritual being and align your mind, body, and Spirit, positive changes will happen, including better health, de-aging, and manifesting things you never thought possible. You can dream again!

Exercise: Identifying Energy & Your Soul

Start the Foundational Meditation for the Day for at least 15 minutes. As you become more practiced, there will be a moment when you can feel that you have shifted and that the mind, body, and soul have aligned. ***This is a 30 to 45-minute practice.***

TIP: Don't push yourselves to see or move too quickly; we call that *"Going into Effort."* Effort is an energy, too, trying to make things happen before their time. You can switch the days up in the week and return to this one; they all work together. No Effort. Let it flow.

While you are in a meditative state with your eyes closed, ask your mind or Spirit to send you an image, sound, or vibration of your soul. Everyone has a different talent to perceive energy, so you might be someone who FEELS it, SEES it, KNOWS it, or HEARS it. It takes practice and will take you several times. Once you connect to this part of your soul, it will be challenging to want to leave this Planet. Because this is your essence, your life force, you will begin to want to fight for its survival with everything you have!

Please note and draw anything you get here; nothing is wrong! Use the sample drawing above to inspire yourself on your soul's appearance. It will change over time as it gets wiser, too!

Draw a Vision of What your soul might look or feel like.

Week 2. Day 2 – Color Flushing

Frequency: Why do we get stuck? Because we have a hard time understanding anything that is not physical anymore. This has been programmed out of the modern human. We are getting it back here! Colors hold energy frequency and tell a story; you must learn how to interpret what they mean. Color-blind people can do this work because it's done in a meditative space. This tool will give you the power to look at life's complexities into your own hands. Here is a quick and brief detailing of color and what each means.

Think of the Rainbow. When you do, most of us think about the brightest versions of these colors, representing the highest energy vibrations. If you see the muted versions of these colors, they also represent something, and here is a quick chart. Please note that some colors might represent something different for you specifically. For example, you are different than what is listed, and when you see "yellow," that makes you think of love or passion, but on this chart, it says those emotions are generally for the color of "red." This is okay, too, and the best part of this work is that it is customized for you. So, feel free to fall into these colors for yourself, creating your specific roadmap.

Unique Color Trick to Note. The most powerful color to blast out negativity might surprise you, but it is BRIGHT YELLOW! Nothing dark can live in this bright color; it is too powerful. If you ever feel overwhelmed by heavy energy, flush your entire being yellow — the most colorful version you can imagine. Pay attention to how you feel; if you can, take note.

Locations/Places. If the energy feels off inside a location, imagine the whole place is this BRIGHT YELLOW, which will shift immediately. You can also run the other colors, but this yellow will give it a quick energy flush.

White Energy	Things can hide in smoky white light and it's why we say "Golden Sun" not White light when we call back our energy. You can look through the white color to learn about what it is. It can mean fatigue or tired energy. White can also mean religious programming or energies that are blocking you from seeing a larger picture. They throw white light onto you to cause confusion and to make you listen to rules. White Energy holds a person back from living their true purpose. Dig in when you see this color and flush it out.
Black Energy	Things can hide in the dark light, and you really need to investigate this color when you see it. This can mean lost, stuck, hidden, sad, depressed, or living in the past or too far into the future and not present, feeling neglected, sorrowful, dejected, disconnected, revengeful.

Black Tar Like Energy	Evil, ancient, or past life energy that is stuck and needs to be healed. Often represented as a time or an energy that had a lot of evil, or dark ritual around it like curses, or a group of people who have been wanting to keep your light down. The light work can pull this off and is no match for this the burning light.
Bright or "Electric" Blue	Communication, cleansing, movement, calm, refreshed, intelligence, focused, determined, tenacious, certain, social, secure, intelligent, intuitive, thoughtful, clear, grounded, nostalgia, irony energy.
Muted/Pale Blue	Masculine energy, low energy, blocked communication, stale, crusty, indecisive, embarrassed, and hesitant energy.
Baby/Soft Blue	Angels, Angelic energy is supporting the outcome, guides, renewed, new Energy coming in like a baby or a child.
Navy/Dark Blue	Male controlling energy, resentment, repressed, abuse, disgusted, dejected, crushed, upset, judgmental, this could be the energy of you, a partner, a family member, or a colleague, or even a past life issue if you ask that question directly.
Bright Pink	Open heart, amusement, laughter, friendship, safety, kindness, compassion, inspired, silliness, comedy, bonding in love or friendship, admiration, safe, trusted, held energy.
Muted/Pale Pink	Feminine energy: low, blocked communication, stale, crusty, jealous, competitive, gossip, criticism. This could be the energy of you, a partner, a family member, colleague or more, shame, perfectionism, embarrassment energy.
Baby/Soft Pink	Stillness, children, innocence, purity, new energy coming in like a baby or a child energy.
Bright Orange	Birth, rebirth, creativity, inspiration, strength, hopeful, excited, living, thankful, optimistic, proud, gleeful, generous, carefree, cheerful, surprised, curiosity, wonder, awe energy.

Muted Orange	Uncertain, worry, dread, vulnerability, repressed creative energy, can't dream, can't express, holding back, not authentic, limited creative energy.
Bright Yellow	Divine connection, light embodied, brave, bold, blissful, personal power, seniority, confident, motivated, invigorated, secure, ambitions, sure, and certain energy.
Muted Yellow (mustard color)	Repressed confidence, potential mental health issues, old wounds creating stuck energy, fear, resentful, fatigue, and exhausted energy.
Bright Green	Spiritually connected and healing of all kinds, abundance, physical healing, energy, thriving, healthy, vibrant, hardy, unique, relaxed, sincere, open-heart energy.
Muted Green	Illness, flu or cold or a viral infection or can represent spiritual sickness, stuck in a pattern, codependency, unhealthy patterns. In life, low vibrational foods, animal energy stuck in body, vain, heartbroken, resentful, critical, uptight, insecurity energy.
Bright Red	Self-love, compassion, passion, love, invigorated, deep physical healing of DNA, ignited, thriving, loving, grateful, pleased, content, boundaries.
Muted or Dark Red	Survival fears around relationships and abundance, anger, livid, mad, raging, annoyed, critical, furious, bitter, suicidal, or homicidal, outrages, heavy, upset, worried, overpowered, afraid, PTSD, past lives death images, powerless, self-pity.
Bright Purple	Intuitive, psychic, informative, education, levity, intelligence, inspired, collective group energy, tribe, community, universal knowledge, all-knowing, guidance, connection.
Muted Purple	Competitive, fraud, envy, nervous, anxious, lonely, lost, fearful, unsure, stubborn, obsessive thinking, humiliated, grief, disenchanted, ashamed, passive, scornful, concerned, disconnected spiritually, programmed to fall into lower vibrations.

Medium Brown	Grounded, calm, peaceful, connected to self and the earth, sleepy, dreamy, open, divine.
Greys	Negative stuck energy, judgment, criticism, energy whacks thrown at you from others, cloudy feeling, darkness stuck in your space, fatigue, sadness, depression, meditations stuck in your space, animal energy stuck from ingestion, controlled energy, past lives stuck.
Silver	Otherworldly energy or information that is not human, extraterrestrials, organism that is not made from this earth plane.
Gold	God's light, the highest form of light, abundance, wealth in all categories, life force energy, Christ force healing energy, highest form of energy to move and transform from any lower vibrational energy.
Violet Energy	This is one of the most transformational energy colors you can use, and it is very powerful. We will use it specifically to transmute physical and mental illness below. This color can deprogram you from other agendas, media, and more. This color with intention can clear spiritual illnesses.

Exercise: Color Flushing

Meditation: Start the Foundational Meditation for the Day for at least 25 minutes, then go to the color flushing for another 20 minutes.

While in meditation, pick a few colors from above that you want to test. Please only do the whole color chart at a time, two maximum a day, and if it's a hard color for you, process only one. You will over-process yourself if you push too hard, which might create momentary panic or anxiousness; if this is happening, it means that it is working, but let's go slow. You can stop and continue later, pace yourself, and only you can know where you are always. For example, if you have a lot of

Navy Blue (primarily male-controlling energy) in your space and you need to process it out, this can be hard going back to childhood (and even in past lives, which we will learn more about later), please only do this one for the day. It becomes fun and exciting to see which colors do what for you.

Congratulations! You are building your intuition and awareness and reading your body and where you are. If you have gotten this far, give yourself a quick pat on the back! It's not easy, and you are showing your strength. Let's keep going.

Goal: Process the low-vibrational colors as much as possible to maintain a higher frequency. Please note that we never get to the point where we are vibrating 100% high all the time. We are still human, and the goal is not to be perfect — there is no such thing. That is a word programmed into our existence — "Perfect!"

Start: Imagine that your entire body, from the very top of your head down to your toes, is this color, everything, yes, everything, all of it! Note the subtle changes in your energy: did it get heavy, light, exhilarating, tingly, emotional, or anxious? Only do this for a few minutes for each color you are testing.

Stop: Say in your head or out loud, *"Please go back to my regular frequency or color."* This will reset you. Give yourself a few "Golden Suns" and recall your life force energy from that color.

Note: Write down below what it felt like.

This is the beginning of color flushing. Future lessons will discuss how to use this even further to rebalance your energy, but for now, this is enough.

Colors Flushed: ______________________________

____

What image or emotion was activated? Note these because they will show wounding and things you might want to work on later.

____

____

____

____

____

____

____

____

Week 2. Day 3 – Rosework, Reading the Energies

Rosework Tool: Why the Rose? Roses are a universal symbol of love and represent you as Spirit. We use the symbol of the rose for most of our work, especially in the beginning, while you are learning to look at your energy. We need a repetitive and consistent container to do work, and this symbol is up for the challenge. Once you know how to use this tool, you can look at anything or anyone in your life and see how the energy works FOR or AGAINST you. You can even tell if someone or a group is lying to you! Now, that is a tool!

STAGES: 1) Closed; 2) Budded but Closed; 3) Beginning to Open; 4) Blooming; 5) In Full bloom.

Exercise: Learning How to Read Your Rose/Energy

Meditation: Start the Foundational Meditation for the Day for at least 15 minutes.

Learn to Ask the Right Questions: This was a challenge for me. I wanted to see what I needed to do, but I could formulate better answers when I looked at specific questions layer by layer. There is no race here; hopefully, you will use this tool for many years.

Practice: While meditative, ask Spirit or yourself, *"Please pull up a rose representing the current state of my energy."* Let that rose appear and look at it in detail.

Is the rose you are looking at opened or closed (using the chart above)?

If you are currently a closed bud, you could be in a hermit mode, closed to a situation or ideas, retracting from people or events, or feeling stuck and needing to heal something. We need to open that rose and get it to full bloom one day. Even doing this work right now, you are starting to encourage yourself to open back up. This is a good thing!

Go to the Rose Below: What are the colors of the rose? Use the sample color chart above to determine what is happening in your rose. Sometimes, this is a solid color, or there are many variations! This should be fun and creative. Now you know! This is your tool!

Ground Your Rose: Now imagine taking the stem of that rose and growing it into the center of the Earth, where the lava is. Say in your head or out loud, *"Please drain or ground all of the energy that is no longer serving me into the lava and burn away."* You might see all the low-vibrational energy start to seep out! Great job.

Give Your Rose a Golden Sun: Now give that rose a giant Golden Sun over the top of it to fill it back up with new energy. You can say, *"Please give this rose a Golden Sun, filling it with my original life force energy, and give me back any energy I might need today. Calling my energy back from people, places, projects, or things!"*

You might be able to see the rose transform right away, or it might even take you a while to see a rose. Don't worry; each has a specific talent. You can't do this wrong. It might take time, which might be hard momentarily if you are emotional. It takes practice like anything else. It doesn't mean it is not happening even if you can't see anything. Just keep trying. Drop that rose and let it burn away.

Practice Rosework.

How are you framing your question? Let's try one about your abundance/money. Try using negative energy first, such as, *"Why don't I have enough money?"* It will show you a rose representing what might be happening in your space, muted colors, female/male controlling energy, or fear. Now, try a new topic and ask this question, *"Why is it so easy to have enough money?"* You will have a different rose, which is the thinking that helps you manifest more money into your life.

Stuck Energy Stopping You from Doing the Work

"I don't want to!"

Yes, a lot of energy stops us from doing the things that are good for us. It's not just the mind that can be an obstacle, but the energy that holds us back. If this is the case, you have some awareness about it; do the grounding meditation, look at this specific energy, and flush it out intentionally. It happens to all of us! Some fears come up with changing, evolving, and removing others from your space that you might be attached to, and the ego is saying this will help people leave you, but that is programming and not valid. As you get shinier, more people will be attracted to you.

Ask for the energy. Do you not like this program? See that energy, flush it out with colors, or put it into the rose and let it release down your grounding cord. If that feels right, create and destroy the roses around it.

TIP: Being Wealthy with the Energy of Money

All money is just an ENERGY! I know this is hard to grasp. But that is all energy; you can have it if your soul prefers it. Spirit wants you to be cared for and wealthy if your soul desires. Money is not an evil thing. Many think they must be poor or broke to learn Spiritual hygiene or alchemy. It is not valid. Now, if you obtain money through means that hurt other people, that is different. If you have an unhealthy relationship with money, where that is your identity, where all your worth is as a human, and your ego is attached to things, that is not good, and that energy should be changed to have a healthy Spirit. If you let money hold a POWER OVER YOUR SOUL, that is not good. Where you might want to take your life because you can't face that you are poor; that is putting money on a pedestal above you. Nothing is above you, not a coin, not a dollar, or anything, or anyone! Release your fears around abundance and money, and watch it come in miraculous ways.

See Mock-ups and Manifesting for more ways to raise your abundance frequency.

Week 2. Day 4 – Transforming Energy/Blowing Roses

We will return to where we were yesterday, but you will learn how to transform those roses and blow the energy here. This energy can be inside you, in others, a relationship that you are in, a family member, a colleague, a project, a job, or anything else that you want to look at and inspect. ***This is a 30- to 45-minute practice.***

How does this relate to being depressed or suicidal or any other mental or physical condition? As you do any of this work, your mind, body, spirit, and soul are getting lighter with more education about how this system works. Every day, you will go through all kinds of ups and downs, but eventually, the ups will start to take over, and they will become more often than the downs.

Go to the questions from the first day and look at their energies with a rose if you need to work on something or continue with what is on your mind.

Exercise: Blowing Roses

Meditation. Start the Foundational Meditation for the Day for at least 15 minutes.

From Week 1, Day 1 section: Rose Protection. 1. Please show yourself the energy you give off to others. 2. What energy do you think you are hiding inside that you need to work on? *Example: "I give off the energy of confidence and expertise, but inside, I feel left out, alone, and judged."* Look at the colors you are seeing and indicate them below. Is the emotion and relation to the color chart above correlating to the answer you wrote down in this first question? You will build your understanding of the colors and how they relate to you reasonably quickly. This can be exhilarating as the colors dance and transform.

Close your eyes and ask questions. *"Please show me a rose that represents my current energy."* Imagine a giant rose with its stem just in front of you, about two feet away. Look at this rose and inspect it. You can use the charts above. Is it open, closed, wilted, burnt, or thriving? Don't worry; whatever you see is excellent one way or the other because by knowing, we can change it fast through this work. Then, inspect the color sequences you see. Is it a solid color, or is it multiple colors? There you are, how simple is that? You are looking at a representation of your current energy. Use the color chart to learn what the colors mean.

What we are doing here is transforming energy. We do that by recognizing the energy, looking at it, holding it momentarily, and actively, with intention, changing it by taking other energy to transmute it into energy that we want or need to have.

See that rose before you, go through the process detailed above, and note what you see or feel below. **DO NOT ADD JUDGMENT or CRITICISM TO YOUR ROSE.** In the beginning, we all have muted colors; it's just energy, and we are transmuting it. Go in gently with yourself. You are here learning unique skills that many people on this Planet couldn't even bother with, so give yourself a massive pat on the back!

What are the colors? Use that same color and blow little rosebuds on your rose. Whatever is the PRIMARY COLOR you are seeing first. Take that color (for example, muted yellow), create tiny little rosebuds that are the same color, and throw them at the rose! Go ahead! Throw them, shower your rose with these little buds, and imagine them EXPLODING! The more extreme, the better; blow them up! This is a reminder to make sure you ground this rose so the energy can drain out! Blow It up!! Keep Going!!!

If you need to put a person's face in the rose, a job, or anything that you feel has stuck energy inside you, you can add them to this rose and blow those roses! I loved this when I first learned it because I am not violent or aggressive, but when I did rosework, I could imagine throwing roses at the energy or people. I was in the driver's seat and changing the power.

Give your rose a Golden Sun. Call in a Golden Sun over your rose or even yourself and recall all your life force energy for this situation or emotion. Stop and drop the rose down your grounding cord when you are ready. Pull up a new rose and see if the energy has changed. It should be a different type of flower and color. It would be best if you did this a few times. After you are done "destroying" the tiny roses, you can drop that rose, just let it fall, create a new one, and look at it to see if it looks any different. It should start to look shinier and brighter and with all colors. Do this often and as much as you want. I practice this in a variety of ways every day. You can do this anytime you need to look at a situation or an energy source, and you want to transmute the energy.

BEFORE & AFTER.

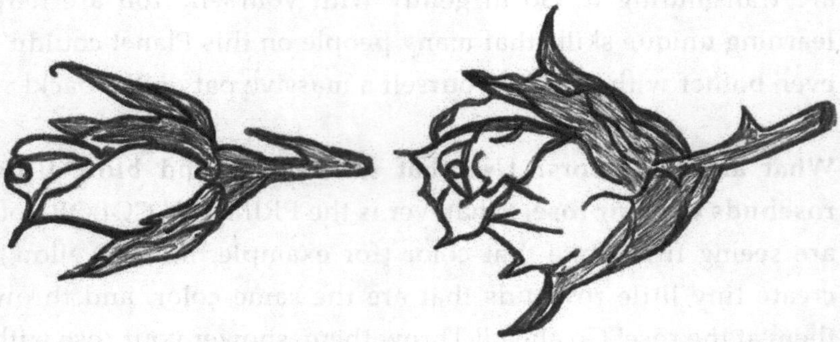

Week 2. Day 5 – Chakra Education, Elements of Being Human

Meditation. Start the Foundational Meditation for the Day for at least 15 minutes.

Now that you have a foundational understanding of colors, we can explore the chakra system. Most people do it the other way around, but learning the colors and what they represent to you is crucial. It should be done first before we dive in and look at the energy centers, but you are ready, and this is the next step.

The chakra (a Sanskrit term for spinning wheel) is an energy and information center within the body that serves as a link or channel for spiritual information. These centers have been found to have a direct relationship with ductless glands and acupuncture points. Many detailed books on this system are available, and detailed recommendations are available in the resource section if you want to go deep into this subject, but we will highlight here the parts you need to do this work.

You are clearing the chakras. Resistance runs through you energetically as stagnation, creating energy blockages in your chakras. This creates a heavy, stuck feeling, making it more challenging to achieve significant changes. It can also cause various misalignments if it persists for long periods. When engaging in meditation and energy work, you can identify where you are holding resistance and work to release it. This work is not intended to change the actual situation in your life but rather how your energy responds to it. These chakras continuously spin unless a blockage stops them from functioning, preventing new information and energy from being stored or processed. They can even be so destroyed that we need to call in an entirely new chakra to be created; this happens when this energy center has been ignored for a long time or abused. Don't worry; there are simple fixes that will give you a brand-new shiny chakra.

Chakra mechanics. The front of the chakra spins clockwise, and the back of the chakra spins counterclockwise. Now, this is something that I rarely see anyone explain. There are twelve circles inside of a chakra (so 11 lines), and they can independently rotate. It's best when they all move in the same direction as intended. Each circle can have its color, frequency, and vibration. All this energy around without ever giving it a warning? By healing and providing these new centers energy, they will reform and begin to work again. We will show you how to do this more in the reading section. The colors represent the energy moving through us and communicating with our chakras in our bodies and Spirits. When you start to see these colors in your space as you meditate, you can focus on whichever form of self-actualization is associated with that color. For instance, if you are seeing green, you can send your energy to your heart center and focus on self-love. You can also choose to use chakra colors to help bring you balance when experiencing suicidal ideation if you are stressed or nervous, opting for soothing colors like green or blue, which balance the heart and throat chakras. If you're depressed, you can boost your mood by wearing red, orange, or yellow to activate your root, sacral, or solar plexus chakras to help you feel more grounded.

The Aura. Stretch your arms above your head towards the sky straight up, then let them fall straight from the sides. That would be a general indicator as to where your aura bubble is around you. As you can imagine, when we are close to people, a lot of people say at a concert or event, our bubbles are all intertwined. If you are a sensitive person energetically and don't know how to clean your energy, you might take home someone or something else's energy. Again, humans have difficulty understanding things they cannot see. That was hardwiring that came into play when "big money" came into human existence and we entered the "Material Age." We are coming out of that into the "Age of Aquarius" and returning to self. It is why many spiritualists, coaches, teachers, researchers, and podcasters feel more open to discussing these matters. It's a great time to be alive. There is so much to learn and understand; you have a front-row seat because you have a beautiful soul in your body.

The Energy Connection—Blue Energy Around the Aura. An electronic blue vibration and zapping energy cycle around the aura bubble. This energy also "connects" to each chakra from the outside of the bubble. We are like walking, talking electromagnetic beings constantly moving energy through our system. This blue light shoots down into the Earth to our lower chakras and up high into the sky to our upper chakras.

Spiritual hygiene and being an atheist. I understand an "atheist" because that is what they chose for this life: to be a total non-believer of energy and spirit, and the goal is to work their way back to spirituality. Many of them, unless they have a near-death experience of something profound, never get there, and most of them (that I have encountered) have harmful illnesses that could have been cured through the idea of "As Above, So Below" that we detail at the top of this chapter. Keep your spirit clean. Remove the lower vibrational energy and fill yourself with this beautiful rainbow energy. Is it any wonder why humans are so low right now? It's one of the hardcore reasons I do this work, as many people are suffering.

I'll use a story to help you understand. I know someone who is an atheist in their mid-thirties and does not believe in Spirit or energy. He primarily watches horror movies and plays video games of a dark nature. He has chosen this life experience, but the goal would have been to break from this stuck thinking to see the beauty of energy and the expansiveness of his soul. Because he has not made the steps towards his learning, he is gaining more and more illnesses to help push him to the edge in hopes that he will turn to awakening and coming online. He has now developed rheumatoid arthritis, colitis, and type 1 diabetes. These are not illnesses that you usually get later in life. I feel for his struggles, but I can see how hard it would be to break from this limited viewpoint of existence. The people in his life reject any energy conversations, so to go another way would be rejecting his family. His journey becomes obvious when written out, but it's hard when you are inside.

Mood stabilizing medications. Many times, people could have been cured through spiritual work but have been talked into going on medications, and some to the point where they are so drugged they can't even connect to their spirit.

People speak about feeling like a "zombie" when on these medications. I asked a friend of mine, who put their eight- and twelve-year-old children on mood stabilizers, if they had taken the medication themselves for a while to see how it made them feel before giving it to their children, and they had not. When I saw one child, he seemed to slur his words. There are more and more studies coming out about these medications. However, some might need them for severe mental health conditions, so it should be the last resort.

Sometimes, people who are very spiritual or have great gifts in this area and do not explore them get scared because they think they are seeing things, but really, they are just gifted in the spiritual sector. Learning how to work the energy and live their best life would be better than medicating them because the spiritual synapses get duller with meditation. If they do have to be on medication, it's our hope they can find a way to run their natural system one day; this energy system will be a big help.

TIP: Your body is more valuable than you know! You can only work on your energy and karma as a soul if you are in your body. Some Spiritual energies would do anything to have your body so they could return and do the work; all they can do is watch you with your body, learn lessons, and transmute energy. No matter where you come from, your station, or your family's appearance, you are here precisely as planned. We will explore this more next month in the exercises of "soul contracts."

Question: For example, the overall color of a chakra can be red, but the circles inside might be grey, blue, pink, or orange. Can you indicate what those colors might suggest if you read the coloring?

Answer: Red — Anger or physical blood that could represent the DNA. Grey — Low vibrational or depression or toxic energy that does not belong to you. Bright blue — high vibrational communication. Muted pink — female controlling stuck energy or joyless. Bright orange — Super high vibrational creative energy.

These chakras can get burnt out to the point where they almost look like they have been burnt or shattered. They are energy centers; they are strong but delicate. It's okay; they need healing and new energy, and you have the tools.

The Chakra System.

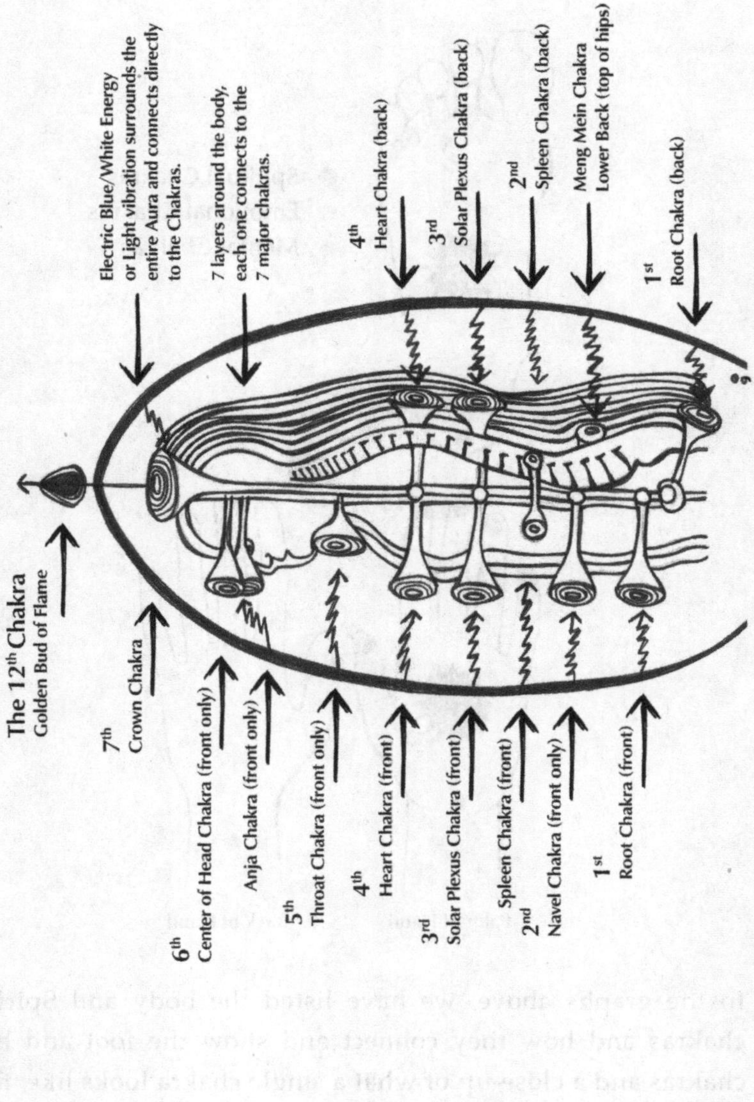

The Hands and Feet Chakra System
(Cavalier, Gina and Amelia Kelley, 2024, pp. 157–160.)

Close up of hand and foot Chakras

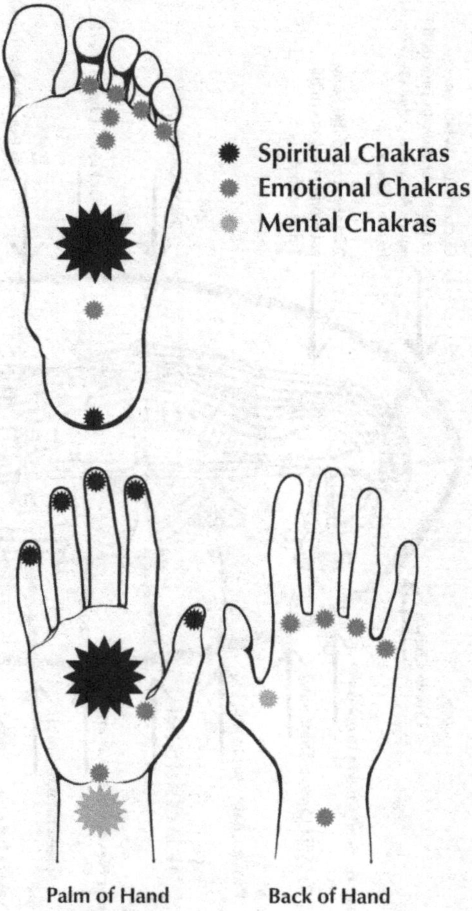

In the graphs above, we have listed the body and Spiritual chakras and how they connect and show the foot and hand chakras and a close-up of what a single chakra looks like; there are a variety of colors running through them depending on where they are in the body and what energy is running through them. There are eleven rings with eleven lines; each ring can move independently. It is best if they are all running in the same direction simultaneously, and this might be why you have heard, *"Your chakras are unbalanced."*

Major chakras. These are the main ones in the body's center that correlate to a specific region and run down the midline or central channel of the body, all the way from the root in the pelvic bowl to the crown of the head, the bottom of the feet, and the hands.

Minor chakras. These small chakras swirl all around you in the body and just above the skin over much of the body, such as the ears, organs, heart, lungs, spleen, eyes, vocal cords, vagus nerves, and more.

There are seven layers around the body. See the image above. The first layer of energy closest to our body correlates to the first chakra. Six more layers relate to each of the major chakras. When we look at a chakra, we can look at it specifically or the entire layer around the body.

Upper- and lower-dimension chakras. Significant chakras in your energy field are below the body, some feet down, above the head, some feet upwards, and connect to universal energy. These are made more aware through deep Spiritual work, and often, people don't learn or connect with these chakras for their entire lives. We are not listing them here, and they will be in more advanced teachings, but they are not necessary for this healing stage.

The Four Elements of Being Human

Each element is affected by the chakra system.

Physical This is the relationship that the chakras have and are affecting the body, your environment, finances, and outward actions like work, friends, and family. Things you can see and feel.
Emotional This is the relationship that you have to your feelings and expressing your emotions, connecting to the wants, desires, needs internally and how you can transform the energy to change it to what you want to feel more of in your life.
Mental This is the relationship you have with receiving and communicating information through your energy systems mostly through the mind in reading, writing, analyzing, and problem-solving.
Spiritual This is the relationship center that connects to your overall well-being and communicating with a higher self and soul and universal knowledge.

Chakra Locations and Descriptions

Chakra Name	Location/ Name	Primary Color	Energy/Description
Aura	All the Skin	All colors	Electromagnetic field surrounding the physical body — protection and safety
Below One	Earth Star	Brown, All colors	Blueprint Mission in Life
In-Body One	Root, Base of the Spine	Red, All colors	**Survival**/Self Preservation/ Anchor/Ignition

In-Body Two	Sacral, by the spleen, three fingers below the navel	Orange, All colors	**Clairsentient:** feeling the emotions of other people/ Creativity/Sexuality/Gratification/ Spark of Life
In-Body Three	Solar Plexus, by the diaphragm, mid-back	Yellow, All colors	Empowerment/Courage/Divine Masculine/Self-Definition **Energy Distribution Throughout the body/Out of Body Experience:** travel when sleeping or in deep meditation **Out of Body Memory:** Past lives
In-Body Four	Heart, Chest, Lungs, at the sternum	Green, All colors	**Affinity**/Physical & Spiritual Meet/Love/Compassion/Doorway to the Divine/Self-Love/Openness/ Bonding/Ability to enter a state of oneness with another person, group, or oneself
In-Body Five	Throat, at the cleft of the throat, and the mouth	Blue, All colors	Communication/Truth/Personal Expression/Humanity/Balance **Clairaudience:** ability to hear beings without their bodies, over a great distance **Inner Voice:** communication between personality and the being **Broad Band Telepathy:** mental communication with groups of people **Narrow Band Telepathy:** mental communication with one or two persons **Pragmatic Intuition:** intuition dealing with practical affairs, e.g. who's calling on the phone, etc.

In-Body Six	Third Eye, the brow or forehead, eyes	Purple, All colors	Precognition/Sensory/Intuition/ Self-Reflection/Clear-sighted Awareness **Clairvoyance:** ability to see mental image pictures, beings without their bodies, auras, chakras, etc. **Abstract Intuition:** ability to arrive at a concept without going through logical processes
Above Seven	The Crown, about an inch above the head, cerebral cortex, pineal gland	Violet, All colors	Precognition/Spiritual Downloads/Dreams/Vision/ Self-Knowledge/Awakening into Greater Realms/Dreamtime **Trance Mediumship:** ability to leave the body and allow another being to enter and act through the body. There are two factors involved, a high degree of genetic programming on a physical level, and a willingness of you the being to leave the body entirely. **Knowingness:** ability to be still and know things that you feel to be true
Hand Chakras		All colors	Psychometry/Healing/Telekinesis
Feet Chakras		All colors	Psychometry/Healing/Telekinesis
Above Eight	Soul Star	White, All colors	Purity/Soul Connection/Cords Deep Encoding Book of Life/ Blueprint of Life
Above Nine	Stellar Gateway	All colors	The Alchemy of the Tree of Life Rainbow Aura Interactive Web of Life/Master of Movement and energy
Above Ten	Galactic	All colors	Radiant Halo of our Higher Self/ Tree of Life Between Heaven and Earth/Medicine Connection

List here some questions you might want to try or additional thoughts about these energy centers and how they might affect your physical, emotional, mental, and Spiritual pathways.

Week 2. Day 6 – Energy Centers/Chakra Reading

Meditation. Start the Foundational Meditation for the Day for at least 30 minutes.

Chakra reading. This technique determines the amount of information or energy a person draws from their chakras, the type of energy within, whether it's their own or someone else's, and more. This process can be done for oneself or others. Practicing this technique may be easier and more enjoyable with others, so feel free to invite friends and family to join in and practice with you.

Source. Our connection to the Supreme Being, Source, or God is profound. We have originated from a divine universal creative energy that bestowed upon us the initial "soul spark" of light from the power of the stars, Planets, and beyond. We will delve into this further in the coming month. Still, this energy is akin to our mother/father, and it loves us, having created all of us and granting us this energy and the wheel of life to evolve into intelligent, resourceful, and magical beings. Various methods can be used to connect with this energy, but the most direct approach is through this manner.

Spiritual protocol/laws to perform readings on others. You need to ask a person if you can perform a reading or healing on another person. There needs to be this agreement somehow, one way or another, to get their permission. Usually, we ask, *"Would you like a healing?"* If they say, "Yes," then you can move forward and do healings and readings on them. This is a common Spiritual courtesy. However, there are a few things you can do without permission that are not an invasion of privacy, which are the following:

- You can pray or send blessings to another person and ask for help, guidance, or Spiritual assistance to help them.
- You can ground them to the center of the Earth.
- You can ask the guides, Spirit, or the Earth energies to help them run their Earth and cosmic energy to release blockages.
- You can give them a Golden Sun of their life force energy back.
- You can connect them to the Supreme Being, Source, God, or Light (whichever you prefer) to provide Spiritual support. We will detail this below.

Start Your Reading/Healing

Don't be overwhelmed by the instructions or their length. Once you understand them, you will run through them quickly — Bing, Bang, Boom! We will also be producing videos on www.theliberatedhealer.com to explain these practices.

The Setup

1. **Meditation.** Start the Foundational Meditation for the Day for at least 25 minutes. This is a little longer because you need to be in an excellent state where your energy runs very fluid. If you are reading someone else, you must ground them and run their energy, along with a Golden Sun for them. Just ask Spirit to do this for you.

2. **Connect to the Supreme Being (description above).** Imagine a thick gold line from your heart that moves through the center of your body, out of the top of your head, and continues up through the Earth's atmosphere to the quiet space and into infinity. Say something like, *"Please connect me to the Supreme Being now."*
3. **Guides.** You can call in any guides who want to be a part of the reading, but you are in charge, so you need to direct them. *"Our guides, high vibrations, Angels, and Light energies are welcome to be with us as we do this work; please start being with me (us) at least 6 feet so you may observe what we are doing and give advice when asked or needed. Thank you."*
4. **Present Time.** Tell the universe you are here in the present, and if you can, write the date on your grounding cord. It would be best if you were here, not traversing the universe.
5. **Chakra Set-up.** Tell Spirit to turn your crown chakra ultimately GOLD. This is setting your antenna to receive. The lower chakras feel the most as they are our survival chakras; during a reading, we must change the energy so our physical body is not overwhelmed. **Females** — Turn down the chakra energy so that 1st is 10% open, 2nd is 10% open, and 3rd is 70% open (when you end and go back to your natural vibration, these will automatically go back when you close the reading). **Males** — Turn down the chakra energy so that 1st is 10% open, 2nd is 10% open, and 3rd is 50% open (when you end and go back to your natural vibration, these will automatically go back when you close the reading).
6. **If you are reading another person, do this now:** If you are reading another person, extend this gold line from your 6th chakra to their 6th chakra, as that is how you read their energy and not your own. You might lose the connection

a few times here and there, but when you stop and re-ground yourself, check your Earth and cosmic energy and ensure that they are running, turn your chakra back to gold, and restart. You will get good at this with practice, where you can reset within a few minutes.

7. **Say an Opening Intention or Prayer.** You can change to the words that most reflect who or what you are, but there needs to be some intentional verbalization or, in the mind of prayer, out into the Spiritual world. Words, actions, and intentions matter. Here is where we sometimes start. If you work with a particular energy, such as Jesus or another figure, you can add the guides and Spiritual energies that make you feel more at peace and safe.

   My Sample of a Prayer:
   "Let us pray: May it be with the blessings of the Supreme Being that whatever happened during this reading/healing help me (or us if you are doing a reading for someone) in our Spiritual growth, awareness, communication, and understanding of who we are and to help transmute those lower vibrational energies that are not a part of our original makeup and send them to the center of the Earth to be burnt away forever. To call in an ample amount of amusement during this process to help move the energies. May I connect to the 'God of My Own Heart' as I am that 'Soul Spark' of this greater universe, and may that light infuse this healing with powerful intention. Thank you, I love you."

8. **Opening communication.** You need to call the soul you are engaging with; if that is you, say your full name, which was on your birth certificate, out loud three times. If this is for someone else, ask them to say their name thrice. If you want another layer, you can ask them to speak

about their date of birth. This tells the universe we are reading, working with this individual soul, and starting communication. **Sometimes, the Spirit is far away from the body.** If you are having difficulty connecting, you must bring that Spirit closer to the body. Ask, *"Spirit, please come back into both fully so we can work."* We are connected by an ethereal cord that keeps us constantly connected to the body until death. There is more on that to learn now or later. With practice, you will see, hear, feel, or know (whatever your specific talent for clairvoyance) when the body and Spirit are together. I will feel and know when that Spirit comes back. I have often seen the Spirit return to the body (it usually comes back into the 7th or 3rd chakra). If a person is very ill or has not practiced much Spirituality, their Spirit might be far away, looking for answers, and a bit traumatized. The body has become a minefield of pain, so the Spirit runs away, trying to collect more information to help itself. See Silver/Clear Etheric Cord for more details on Day 7's education.

Reading Your Rose

Use the above tools: *Chakra chart, Rose Charts and Drawings, and the Color Chart.*

1. **General Reading: Please pull up a rose that represents the readee's current energy in this life and ground it to the center of the Earth.** Look at the rose from all sides.
   a. Is the rose open or closed? It would be easy to tell, much like when we learned about looking at the rose. Are they open and in full bloom in their energy, or are they a shut bud? We want to be open and in full bloom, in our best energy, and to live and manifest the life we most desire.

b. What colors are flowing through the rose? Dig in and look around from all sides. Use the color chart to determine the energy and tell the readee or yourself what you see.
c. Does the rose have a long or short stem? If the stem is long and goes on for a long time, that would indicate that the soul is very old. The stem should have rings from the top to the end, which might have different colors. These rings will represent a single life that their soul was engaged in. You might see that one of the rings is vibrating or being highlighted somehow. That would indicate that past life wants to provide information that will help the readee today. If not, the soul might be shy, and it will come out next time. If you don't see anything, it does not mean it is not there; it's just that you must practice. If you see a ring you want to look at, we will dive into the "Past Life Reading," if not, go directly to the "Main Chakra Reading."
d. Does the rose have any leaves on the stem? If so, these leaves represent their contracts to parent a child in one way or another.

Your Practice Rose.

God of Your Heart Reading

Now imagine a big sun behind that rose and look at the placement of the sun. The sun represents the God of your Heart, your true-life purpose, and everything proper for you — your soul's information. The relationship of the rose to the sun represents your communication with God: Are you looking toward the God of Your Heart for your information, or are you looking away from the God of Your Heart? The openness of the rose indicates how open you are to this communication.

The Rose. It represents you as Spirit; the Sun represents the God of Your Heart — all those things that are true for you – your spiritual information.

The Relationship. The rose to the Sun represents your communication with God. Are you looking towards the God of your Heart for information, or are you looking away from the God of your heart? The rose's openness indicates how open you are to this communication.

The Path. Are you on your path? If the rose is directly underneath the sun (6 o'clock in relation to the sun), then yes. If not, you know how far off you are on your soul's true journey.

The Stem of the Rose. The stem length indicates how long you've taken bodies on this Planet. If the stem goes to the bottom of the page and has roots, you have been here since the beginning of the Planet. Breaks in the stem indicate a time when you went to another universe.

Past Lives on the Stem. You have past lives all along the stem of the rose. During this lifetime, you will have times when you access your past life information for whatever reason. The past lives you currently access show up as rings (like Saturn) around the stem. The rings towards the hip of the rose are more recent than those towards the bottom of the stem, which are longer ago.

Spiritual Children Contracts. These appear as leaves on the stem of the rose, one leaf for each agreement. This is not a prediction of children; it is only an indication that there are spirits out there that you have agreed to have as children sometime (not necessarily this lifetime).

Past Life Reading (60-minutes)

We only suggest doing two past lives at a time. They come up and into your space so you can look at the information and things you learned in that life that can help you where you are today. When you do this, you are processing that life, and it will roll out for the coming weeks the karma or dharma you received in that life. For example, if you have been very depressed in this life and you are not sure why, this life will show you something that helps you better understand why you might be depressed. You are a whole being with many stories. We are processing not just the stories from this life or today. As we reveal all this information, your Spirit is lightening, connecting you more to the universal knowledge and your deep meaning as an individual soul.

The Ring that is Highlighted. Let's look at the first ring that is highlighted. Be an Investigator!

1. Where is the ring in relation to the rosebud? If it is close to the bud, that means it was more recent, and if it's very far down, that means it was sometime back in your history.
2. What color is the life being highlighted? That gives you the initial energy of that life, but it might relate to its physical, emotional, mental, or Spiritual aspects. You need to figure it out through examination and investigation.
   a. Use the Color Charts, for example — Orange/Creative, Blue/Communication or Business, Purple/Visionary, White/Religious teacher or guru, Red/Warrior, or Doctor. OR it might want to communicate what was in that life we need to look at as the emotion.
   b. Ask why this life is being shown and what is the core reminder or communication you need to see today. Journal this yourself or communicate anything you see, hear, or feel to the readee. Ask more questions:
      i. What is the timeline of this life – see what you hear?
      ii. Look at the people's clothes or ask to see them.
      iii. Who is in the image? Does it look like this life shows your reader as a male or a female?
      iv. Were they wealthy or struggling? Who were the other people around?
      v. Are there any animals in the image?
      vi. Are you on land or water?
      vii. What is the circumstance you are in?
      viii. Why is this being shown? What lesson is here to remind you today of what you need?
      ix. What are the emotions of the people in the scene?

3. You will start to get a storyline, and it might take a few asks to determine the core lesson. For example, you might see a capsized boat, and you are hanging on and getting ready to pass. Then, you open a locket and see your one true love, who looks like someone you know. That might be a sign that they are your soulmate, and you should lean into getting to know them better. The stories are endless, and they are all beautiful. Once you have gotten your messages, move on and clear some energy.
4. **Ground that life and give it a Golden Sun.** Now you are healing that life and say, "Recalling all the original life force energy back to the soul from this life."
5. **Ask the readee if you have a question that they would like to ask or know about this life.** This takes practice, so take your time, even being patient with yourself. This practice is teaching you valuable life lessons. All good things come to those who wait and can harness patience. You all have these skills. They might differ slightly, but we can all do this work.
6. **Return to the rose, look at the next life, and repeat the above steps.**
7. **Close out this part of the reading.** When you are done with the past lives, re-ground the rose and give it a Golden Sun, re-ground the readee or yourself, and ensure all the energy is running. Drop that rose into the center of the Earth or blow it up and let it go down the grounding cord to burn away.

Main Chakra Reading

Remember, we are here to have fun and read energy. Don't get too serious about this, and if you do, create a fake laugh, which is an actual technique, "Ha, Ha, Ha, Ha, Ha, Ha." It's there to break up anytime the energy gets too severe.

Use the above tools: *Chakra chart, Rose Charts and Drawings, and the Color Chart.*

1. **Set yourself back up.** Go through steps 1–8 again in the setup section.
2. **Aura.** The aura is created from a blend of the energies flowing through all the chakras. Can you see the large aura around the body at all? This might take practice, but if you see, feel, hear, or know anything, say it out loud. Don't contemplate too hard about what you are seeing. People sometimes stop because they might see something they are doubting is real. That will shut the energy down; go with the flow.
3. **Look at the 1st chakra or the 1st layer.** You can say out loud or in your mind, *"Let's look at chakra 1, the root chakra."* You will start to see, feel, or hear things so you can begin to pay attention. The first color that comes to your mind's eye is the primary color in the chakra. This area of the body is the closest to the body and usually reflects the general well-being of the body and primarily physical things that might be going on.
4. **Suppose you are still waiting to get something.** Start to blow miniature roses on the chakra that you are reviewing. There could be resistance from you or the readee if there is one. This will break up the energy, and you will start getting something. Go ahead and look at what you are seeing. Seeing a lot of grey or dark red means other people's energy is in there, and so is anger (use the color chart). Blow the energy with the roses and let it transmute. You might start to see a vision.
5. **Read what is coming up.** What are the colors coming up? How does it feel? Explore it and start to ask questions, go into the visuals or sounds. There are many layers upon layers; keep going farther and farther. Continue to blow

roses when you can, as that is helping to heal the chakra. Since the person has already been grounded and running the energy, they are already in a healing phase. You are working on this one chakra right now. Have fun, learn, grow, and experience.

6. **Recall the energy.** Give yourself or the readee a Golden Sun, recalling the energy for that chakra only. You will see the energy dump into the person and go straight to that chakra! You just healed yourself or another. You should be so proud of yourself! You are transforming yourself and the world.
7. **Look at the 2nd chakra or the 2nd layer.** This area is tied to communication about how it experiences the energy around it – like the person's emotions. A lot of information about relationships is in here, including past abuse or weighty emotional things. A lot of people might start to tear up during this chakra healing. Read, blow roses, and give it a Golden Sun.
8. **Look at the 3rd chakra or the 3rd layer.** This area relates to how the body gets things done, how we manifest things in our lives, how we connect to our Spiritual beings, and what plans we put into action. Read, blow roses, and give it a Golden Sun.
9. **Look at the 4th chakra or the 4th layer.** This area is related to our affinity; it's the communication between the physical and Spiritual layers of the aura. Grief and heartache will be in this space. Read, blow roses, and give it a Golden Sun.
10. **Look at the 5th chakra or the 5th layer.** This area is related to creativity and speaking (or not speaking) your authentic views in life. A person might get choked up when you work in this area, which may give them the courage to step more into their seniority. Read, blow roses, and give it a Golden Sun.

11. **Look at the 6th chakra or the 6th layer.** This area is where we lean into our awareness, intuition, vision, and clairvoyance. There is also a lot of programming from other people, governments, or companies here. How do we know what we truly want when all this information exists? This will free you. Read, blow roses, and give it a Golden Sun.
12. **Look at the 7th chakra or the 7th layer.** This area is related to our Spirituality, our contracts, our guides, and who we are as a Spirit. Read, blow roses, and give it a Golden Sun.

Close out the reading. If you are reading someone else, you can let them go; if not, you must close this process.

Imagine a giant old book opening. Write the name of the person in the book, and imagine all the images, thoughts, and anything from the reading/healing being put inside the book. Close the book and say in your head or aloud, *"End of healing, end of reading, end of communication."*

Ground and Golden Sun. Drop your grounding cord and give yourself a new one and a final sizeable Golden Sun.

Congratulations, you are a liberated healer!

Example/Tip:

I was doing a reading for a client, and I was in her 5th (throat) and 6th (center of the head) chakras. I kept getting images and feelings of mushrooms or something that looked like them. I had to dig deep; what was this? Maybe she was allergic to mushrooms? I asked where the mushrooms were and saw a kitchen in an apartment, which showed me that it was in a wall. Together, we figured out that it was mold in her apartment, and it was making her and her animals sick. They had a mold inspector come out, and she had to move out in an emergency as she and her animals were getting permanent damage. Thank goodness she came for a healing, and I could see that. Healings are remarkable and always make you and the other person feel great. Something is always better and transformative.

Week 2. Day 7 – Integration Day, Etheric Cord, Changes Happening

Meditation. Start the Foundational Meditation for the Day for at least 15 minutes.

That was a huge week, and we learned a lot. We will invest more in education and ways to help you move through this Planet, including physical and mental illnesses, but you need to learn tools straight away to set yourself up right.

Silver/Clear Etheric Cord (Spirit and Body connection)
A thin translucent cord connects your Spiritual/astral body to your physical body through the vibratory field. Other mystics have often called this the "Silver Cord," but it has no color. It's just that when the energy glistens, it gives a silver sheen. This refers to my teaching in my first book, as I, too, made this mistake but have been corrected by Spirit.

Your SPIRIT never sleeps. The body does so often. When you are in a deep sleep, your Spirit will go far away in search of other souls, information, or learning. If you suddenly wake up and feel strange, it might be because it takes a while for the Spirit to return to your body. You can call your Spirit to come back right away; ask it! Your Spirit is strong and will do almost anything you ask if it's Spiritually able.

When you pass, the angel of death, Azrael (or other angels under him), comes and takes their large scythe and cuts the cord, thus making the body unanimated. The soul will start to lift, looking like dust or stardust particles. We will go into this more in the Spirit Guide sections. He has a black cape on, so you can't see him coming so as not to scare people (which is the opposite of how movies have shown it). Inside the cape is the bright white light of an angelic spirit that helps take people home. We all go home; we are all a part of this giant tapestry of life in things like a spiritual matrix.

Spiritual Law #1. Everything Changes

Please note that things change in this world. How we look at things changes, the world changes, and even the rules of Spiritual engagement can change; things that are no longer useful can be retired when they are no longer working or needed. There WILL BE things in this book that change and shift. That is every living thing in nature. It is why people have such a hard time when they stick so hard and fast to rules. This is hard to articulate because humans love being right, not wrong. If they change, then they have this energy that they were terrible before. These anxieties and the ego create fear, but we can redirect that now that we know.

The question is, what rings true or correct for you now? Not in the future, not in the past, but now. If you over-analyze the content too much and look for "proof," that is a sign it's not resonating with you; that is okay. Just move away from that and go to the things that ring for you. Even at the end of the day, if all of this was, in fact, not true, if it helped you and maybe someone else who is suffering and, for example, thinking about ending their life ... wouldn't that have been a significant enough reward?

When someone says, "I dislike change," I get it, but change is necessary to grow, which is why this is the first lesson. Often, we hesitate to change because we are afraid of the outcome. This builds a callous resistance around our energetic space. We age faster, take on heavier energy, get intense illnesses, and get energetically stuck.

In this image, the spirit world is all around us,
and in the pool's reflection, there is an image
of a ghost standing next to the girl.

Ghosts

The existence of ghosts is a topic that I find fascinating. I've written an entire screenplay about a ghost who carried with her a rich and poignant life story and sought healing on the "other side." In my understanding, when a ghost is present, it signifies that a part of it is tethered to this realm due to a traumatic departure, leaving an energetic imprint in the lower dimension. Ghosts require energy, which can be drawn from humans, electrical devices, or batteries, to interact with the physical world. This explains phenomena such as sudden cell phone battery drain or electronic interference in their vicinity. However, manipulating physical objects from the other side demands considerable effort and swiftly depletes their energy reserves, rendering them inert for a significant period afterward.

Most ghosts seem trapped in a cycle of reenacting a distressing moment and possess limited awareness of their current state or purpose for lingering. Encountering a ghost with the ability to communicate and engage with the living effectively is scarce. In these cases, they possess some consciousness about their situation and have consciously chosen to remain in this transitional state, albeit in a portion of their being. Guiding such ghosts toward the light and elucidating the benefits of transitioning enables them to achieve wholeness once more. Many spirits harbor fears associated with the afterlife, such as relinquishing their connection to a beloved family member or facing retribution for past misdeeds. Despite their worries, it's crucial to acknowledge that all souls possess free will, and their decision to linger on this plane is self-imposed. Transitioning to the afterlife allows them to confront their inner turmoil and commence the healing process.

Our role in assisting these spirits primarily revolves around illuminating the path to the afterlife, as they often seem to have lost sight of this guiding light. We aim to impart an understanding of what awaits them beyond this realm — a place of pure love and belonging, akin to finding one's true home. It's important to note that such communicative and aware spirits are rare. Even if we succeed in guiding them to the light, it's unlikely that they will remain connected to our vibrational frequency or that of our family. However, there are instances where these enlightened spirits may check in on us as part of our spiritual support team. For example, if a loved one has passed away, their soul remains accessible to us and can be invoked simply by calling out their name.

These transcended spirits exist beyond the realm of ghosts, returned to the timeless and ethereal plane of existence that we call the universe of the souls, significantly distinct from the notion of being tethered to Earth.

I used to be intrigued by TV shows attempting to prove the existence of ghosts, but I've come to realize that such content may need to be healthier. It feels like they're exploiting the spirits, trying to force them to perform unnaturally. If they genuinely want to help, they should guide the spirits to ascend and find peace.

Here's a personal story that reinforced my beliefs. I had a beloved dog named Milo, whom I adopted from a shelter when he was around a year old. He was a mix of Labrador and Chow, and he had experienced some trauma before coming to me. Initially, he was so broken that he wouldn't even lift his head. However, as we delved into spiritual healing, Milo would always stand by my side, almost as if he were holding space for the healing process. We affectionately referred to him as the "Shaman dog."

Orbs

Orbs are spirits and passed over loved ones, guides, or angels. They are in a circle because they are encapsulated in one complete element with no beginning and no end. They light this because they can move fast and bio-locate to you when needed. Sometimes you might see a face inside of the orb. They are coming to visit us.

Proof of Soul/Ghosts with an Animal

When Milo passed away, something remarkable happened. The morning after his passing, the doorbell rang at our usual waking time of 7:30 am. Upon reviewing the footage captured by the Ring doorbell, I noticed a surreal sight. No one was at the door, but I could see gold sparks, a wagging tail, and a bright, shining soul, unmistakably Milo. He rang the doorbell every morning, gradually transforming into a larger, brighter ball of light.

After one week, Milo's ashes were delivered to me, and I could sense that he felt safe leaving us. His visits became less frequent and eventually ceased altogether. Although he still occasionally manifests during our healing sessions, I know he has found peace. Milo was undoubtedly with us that week, waiting to be reunited and feel at home again.

Milo the Shaman Dog (lived to be 18 years old).

Milo rang the Ring camera doorbell the following day and every day for a week until his ashes returned home, and you can see his soul to the right. You could see the tail in the back waving in the video and coming from what looked like the sky downward. I still have the video.

Neo, Simon, and I hanging out with Milo in the morning.

Milo's soul was getting more formed each day for seven days straight as his soul was healing and getting collected. When we got his ashes on the 7th day and once, he was home, the Ring camera never rang again, and his soul had left this plane, and he was back home to spirit.

HORSE – Week 3 – Re-Education Begins: Light and Dark, Soul Blueprints, Guides, Angels, Entities, Guardians, Remove Dark Energy

This week, the White Horse is our Spirit Animal, and an Earth Angel shows itself.

"The horse is one of the most majestic Spirits in the world; they love and fear us simultaneously because they are so sensitive to our every emotion. We are complex creatures, and we (the collective horse energy) are happy to see a book like this. They will offer their energy, strength, freedom from programming, guidance, wild abandon, courage, and Fortitude. The Earth Angel is a warrior of Spirit, showing us how to remove the darkness and fly into the light again."

Week 3. Day 1 – Free Will/Consciousness, Spiritual Laws, Light and Dark Energy Education

Meditation. Start the Foundational Meditation for the Day for at least 15 minutes.

This is not easy work, and you have made it to week 3 of the program and are in the middle of your hyper-re-education of the human existence of your physical, spiritual, emotional, and mental self. Although it is work, we hope you still find it enlightening and fun to explore your soul. You needed the above tools before we dove headfirst into what takes us away from our path and where many fears and rewards lie hidden in each of us.

Free Will/Consciousness

The Planet is alive and started as a large cold rock, and over time, the planet aligned with the sun, and the moon could begin to grow many living beings. They rose with the source consciousness, a powerful and creative energy that holds information and power from multiple universes. It also dances in light, dark, love, and fear. Over time, this source continues to learn itself and make changes when needed, using the dance of creativity to birth new ideas and life. As humans started to evolve, so did their consciousness and intelligence.

Adam and Eve. The story of Adam and Eve holds deep meaning for us as it signifies a turning point in human existence. It was decided by a multilayered source consciousness that humans needed to be more connected to the broader consciousness and should have the free will to make their own decisions. Despite knowing that humans would face numerous challenges and might stray from the right path, they were believed to learn and evolve, ultimately creating a utopian society on our beautiful planet, Earth. However, at that time, the universal consciousness energy had not foreseen the occurrence of human conflict and war. It's hard to fathom that humans would choose to create turmoil on a planet with such astonishing natural beauty, including diverse ecosystems of mountains, oceans, plants, animals, insects, and more.

Upgraded consciousness here. The children born around 2019 exhibit a higher level of awareness than previous generations. This heightened consciousness is believed to connect them with their past lives and is an intricate system detailed in their Akashic Records (which will be explained in later chapters). It is said that this decision was influenced by a higher authority and a council with a galactic perspective aiming to support humanity. The typical way most of us enter this world involves a lack of memory regarding our past lives, cosmic understanding, and connection to a higher source. It was believed that having this knowledge handed to us would hinder our growth and learning, akin to receiving answers to a test. Thus, it has been decided that the future of humanity requires more consciousness and intelligence. This may lead to an increase in exceptional individuals such as savants, prodigies, and children with vivid recollections of their past lives.

Fact: Humans created WAR. The primary origins of the central wars can be traced back to the creation of a monetary system that led to the development of class divisions and a range of negative emotions such as jealousy, resentment, criticism, shame, and judgment. Since then, efforts have been made by the source consciousness to eliminate war, but due to our free will, it can only offer support. However, whenever war subsides in one area, it resurfaces in another. It is essential for a collective effort to bring about significant change. The solution lies in doing the inner work, understanding one's energy and soul, and striving to live a purposeful life while inspiring others to do the same. It's about discovering what ignites your soul and embracing it with unwavering determination, even fearing failure, love, or unpopularity.

As you connect and collapse into one — the mind, body, spirit, and soul — you will become a beacon of light and a transformative human. Your one soul can help change the world. Some of this work is how we do it, and it's a great start.

Dark and (trickster) Entities and Spells

Yes, unfortunately, there are opposing forces in the world, but they operate on a completely different frequency. As we've learned, words and rituals have the power to create positive energy, but they can also manifest darkness. The key is not to fuel it with your energy, respect, or fear. Always return to love because these forces thrive on instilling fear. By not acknowledging their power, you strip them of their energy. You are the one who can control whether this energy is allowed to come in or not. If you allow it in on purpose through dark ritual, you will give your light away and begin to forget your true purpose here, which is to be all love. You can change it instantly, by going back to love and rejecting this energy.

Exercise to be Rid of this energy:

Use the vision of a bright white flame of light getting bigger and stronger and visualize the dark energy falling away from you and to the center of the Earth and burning away and address the energy by declaring, "I am not a victim of you; I am a sovereign being, and your energy holds no sway over me." You can also invoke the protection and assistance of an ascended master like Jesus, and their presence will shield you and dispel the negative energy.

Sigh loudly and hold onto the vibration in your chest, "OM, OM, OM, OM, OM, OM." The OM frequency can put power into the flame to give you great strength and will flush out the dark. Source energy uses "sound" to create intense light and lies inside the spaces between the breaths to push it through.

Call upon the ascended masters as equals to you now walking together. Your oversoul will integrate this knowledge and experience and this tool will now be a part of your healing toolkit for yourself and others. Honor and respect yourself and this journey once again. You are strength and you have tamed a lion with love.

Spiritual Laws. There are five spiritual laws that we can identify. We know that sounds like a short list, but if you read them below, you should know they are true. Humans were not meant to be painted into a box. Teaching is critical because we are all students and must have teachers. If there are lessons and texts to teach us, that is very different from the **rules** put on us where we are told to follow them. A person's soul contract might be that they must be raised with those rules, only to break free and learn that they don't have to live under those limitations, which is a part of their soul-requested journey, and even this should not be judged. Let them know, let them grow — let us learn, let us grow, we will let you understand, and let you grow — with love.

Physical Death. When one passes, they get to see the whole of their life, and we will explain much more later under life review.

The 5 Universal Spiritual Laws

I had a reading in October 2021 with Bashar, an ET from the Planet Essassani who is said to be 300 years into the future and channeled by Darryl Anka. He gave me the following Universal Spiritual Laws, and to this day, I have not found anything better than these laws. I believe these to be true, so I am including them here. Before you venture out, it's essential to know how not to step on others' spiritual toes (Bashar/Anka, n.d.).

Spiritual Laws:

1. You Exist (and there isn't anything you can do to change that; even if you decide to leave the Planet, your soul will still exist).
2. Everything is the Here and the Now (and there isn't anything you can do to change that).
3. The one is all, and all is the one (we are all connected as one conscious, so working out how to get along more instead of dividing groups will make us all happier).
4. What you put out is what you get back (if you put out good energy, you get good results).
5. Everything is constantly changing except these laws.

Week 3. Day 2 – Calming Meditations/Exercise

We will get into more intense subject matter that might rattle what you've known your whole life. Here are a few easy to go to meditations to bring in the calm.

"I am Joy Meditation." This meditation is performed standing to allow energy to flow freely, bringing you back fully into your power. If you are unable to stand, choose any position that feels comfortable. Set the environment with calming natural lights or candles.

- Stand barefoot to better connect with the Earth, with your feet hips-distance apart.
- Keep your eyes open; this helps you remain present with your mind and body connection.
- Stand tall and pull your shoulder blades back toward each other, opening your heart space.
- Pull your hips or buttocks back to help align yourself, reset the natural S curve in the spine, and support your lower back.
- Keep your knees slightly bent (not locked).

Imagine a white string moving from the base of your spine up through the center of your body and out the top of your head to the clouds and then downward into the Earth below.

- Take three deep breaths into the nose, expanding your diaphragm, and exhale the air out of your mouth.
- Return to natural breathing.
- Let your arms rest at your sides with your palms faced outward, open to receive.
- Tuck your chin to your chest and roll your head toward the left three times and then to the right three times.
- Relax your jaw and close your eyes.

- Imagine a giant Golden Sun on the back of your shoulders growing larger and larger as it fills you with liquid joy. When the sun is large enough, allow it to burst and cover your entire being.
- Say out loud, "I am joy." Repeat this with conviction and repeat the Golden Sun cycle at least three or more times.
- Raise your arms overhead and stretch them to the sky if you can. Fold your fingers in on each other, forming a steeple, and let your head fall back gently, giving way to a slight back bend.
- Return your head to neutral and slowly fold yourself toward your toes, reaching for the ground. Imagine any weight you carry falling off your shoulders and out the crown of your head into the Earth.
- Roll yourself up slowly, bringing your head up last.
- Allow yourself to smile if it feels good and say again, "I am joy."

Breathing Exercise (Rainbow/Fire & Gold/Silver)

Meditation. Start the Foundational Meditation for the Day for at least 15 minutes.
This is a simple breathing meditation that is very effective. You will feel blockages removed and lighter, as well as even a little Kundalini energy, which is a particular technique to awaken your root chakra, but that would be a side effect and not its primary function.

IN: The rainbow is the high vibrational color of the universe.
OUT: The fire is the anger, pain, suffering, competition, sadness, and wounds.

IN: The gold is the high vibrational light of Source, God, cleansing, and joy.

OUT: The silver is the low-vibrational energy that has been stuck and others' energy, judgments, and criticisms that you or others have added to your space.

Breath is the source of all life. Without the very air that we breathe, none of these matters. Many books go deep into why breathing work is so vital, and we will list them in the resource section. For us, the air is a tool that moves through our physical body to release blockages and energy so we can let the good energy in. We respect it as the key to our animation.

Breath Work. Breathe in for four seconds, hold for four seconds, breathing out for four seconds.
Why eight times? It is the symbol of universal infinity, connecting us all.

8 Times: Breathe in Rainbows (highest vibration of color you can imagine). Breathe out Fire (see, feel, and hear the fire coming out).

8 Times: Breathe in Gold (highest vibration of color you can imagine). Breathe out Silver (see, feel, and hear the fire coming out).

Quick Breaths. Then, breathe and blow in and out quickly for 20–30 seconds to reset your 1st root chakra.

Golden Sun. Call back your energy to fill yourself back up.

Week 3. Day 3 – The Lighter Side of Life

Meditation. Start the Foundational Meditation for the Day for at least 15 minutes.

The Spirits of Light and Dark are not at odds with each other. Light and dark are not at war with one another. Instead, they playfully entangle and spiral with one another. Sometimes, light is on top; sometimes, darkness is on top. That is the genuine relationship of light and dark.

The Light Source. The essence of love resides within each living being on this planet, a "soul spark" drawn from the cosmic fabric of the universe and the stars. When I connect with energies or angels, they often emphasize our limited way of thinking, particularly our use of language. They stress the need for more words that convey love. Love is the primary ingredient, encompassing even those we harbor disdain for. Our soul is our most precious possession, which we must nurture and safeguard. The light within us is akin to the love of countless mothers. It explains why many feel the urge to leave and why thoughts of self-harm pervade our minds – we long to return to our true home, which feels like a safe, nurturing, and understanding sanctuary akin to a womb.

Everywhere, all at once. All humans are integrated with this essence of the light and the dark, although the specifics elude us. We have access to all these energy sources and their associated knowledge, which the universe shares. Together, our collective presence is more impactful than individual separateness. Simultaneously, we possess a universal uniqueness that sets us apart. Planet Earth is the most magical ball of energy that has ever been birthed, along with more DNA and species than anywhere else in all the universes. We must know that we are unique even to get here. Once you see your magic, you can never unsee it, and then you will know how special you are and what you can achieve in this one perfect version of you. Please don't discount your value; you are here.

A spiritual war. Humans can energetically create Gods of energy. On the human level, though, where gods can be made and Earthed, these types of egregores and archetypal representations of light and dark can come into existence and interact with human beings. How many people have been visited by the Devil and by God or their representatives? Some of them are very relevant and active here, but many of them are human-based and created. As we mentioned in the beginning, we are not here to pinpoint religious points or explain the energies that we work with to heal. There are far more qualified books and persons who can speak about this important figure in our human culture and how we walk on Planet Earth.

Jesus Christ was a human man, directly from God or Source, brought here to show humans the purest form of love. He is, in our eyes, the original healer. His energy has transformed from human to a particular healing consciousness, and this healing energy can be everywhere at once and called upon to assist at a moment's notice. Whether you can see, hear, feel, or know and ask for the healing of Jesus Christ, that energy will come in no matter what. That does not mean that you might experience a spontaneous miracle (which is possible), but his healing source energy will and can be called upon and directed where you need it to go. In further chapters, we will explore the contracts we created for our souls to experience next week. Because of this, we need to learn things that are usually not the most pleasant. These are complicated to explain, and why there are many thousands and maybe even millions of books and texts in this category, but most people agree that humans have **FREE WILL**.

Exercise — Christ Force Energy Healing

Meditation. Start the Foundational Meditation for the Day for at least 15 minutes. If you do this on another person, you can ground them and run their energy if they do not know how.

Activate hand chakras. As you meditate, energy fountains out of your hand chakras, and you feel grounded and calm. Raise your hands with your fingers apart. Say the following in your head or aloud: "Christ, force healing. Please come into my hand *chakras*."

Unground. Remove the grounding cord for you or the other person who is getting the healing. You will be asked to be ungrounded very few times, but this is one of them, and we will show you why.

Go to the feet. Grab the bottom of the feet with your hand chakras in the middle of both foot chakras. Command, "Christ, force energy. Please enter and begin to heal." It is best to do this to others, if possible, but if you are doing this to yourself, then grab your feet. The reason is that lying flat and not having any bent limbs helps move this energy smoothly.

Imagine gold lava. Christ's force energy is like gold lava, and it will enter the feet. It moves slowly, so it's best to try and imagine it going up the shins, past the knees, through the thighs and the organs, around the heart and lungs, spine, through the throat, up over the face, and down the arms to shoot out of the top of the head through the 7th crown chakra. Let this run for a few solid minutes with no stopping. It is a massive clearing of the chakras and spiritual attachments in the body. **You will know when it is time to stop.**

Re-ground the body with an extensive grounding cord and Golden Sun. Imagine all this lava falling through the grounding cord and sending it to the center of the Earth into the lava so it can be burnt away. Add plenty of Golden Suns with all kinds of colors if you can.

Unplug. Ask that your hand chakras be returned to their regular frequency.

The best part: When you heal someone else, you also heal. This is partly because we have shared wounds or past lives. When we do something to help another, there is no better gift. If you do something to help someone who has done terrible things to you or even forgive them, you will significantly lighten your load. We will talk about this more in the karma section.

Please note here any images you saw, heard, felt, or learned as a "knowing."

____

____

Week 3. Day 4 – The Darker Side of Life Education

The Shadow – The Gradient between light and dark

In the realm of shadow work, we embark on a profound inner journey akin to competing in the Olympics of our soul. We aim to emerge as valiant warriors capable of maintaining the delicate equilibrium between light and darkness within ourselves. Each soul is tasked with its own "Hero's Journey," a narrative of triumph over personal challenges. This book and other forms of expression equip us with the skills and tools necessary for this endeavor. It's essential to remain receptive to messages that resonate with our hearts, whether written or spoken. Even one sentence can ignite our most profound memories and lead us to realize that we are divine beings, always have been and always will be. Here's to us, here's to you — let's do this together!

Healing Suicidal Ideation – Shadow Work

This is a channeled list from our guides on this book to consider as you go through the needed shadow and life work. A few lines will speak to the individual. Highlight yours with a marker, embrace it, and then try another later in your journey, eventually getting through all of them by the end of your life here on the Planet. We will do this work through meditation, pendulum, or rosework.

Start a meditation you prefer for at least 30 minutes and do the rosework around these shadow energies.

- Try to look at people with a sign on them that says, "Say something nice to me."
- Consider the realities of suicide and its aftermath for the people left behind.
- Healing is a solo sport. You can make your life better. You've heard stories — and why they get out there — of people with incredible odds of changing their lives or accomplishing a great goal. Even though it's a solo sport, you have a lot of support.
- Remember the beautiful things about your soul and journey and how much you can accomplish here.
- Tribe values belonging — seek happiness through the tribe.
- Change our understanding of suicide.
- Depression is a symptom, not a malfunction.
- Withdrawn from your senses and confusion, let your spirit drive sometimes.
- Every choice you make either enhances your experience or drains it.
- Don't betray what is in your heart.
- Change your focus. You might be focused on something or someone that wasn't right for you. It's okay; permit yourself to walk away.

- Avoid the phrase "you shouldn't have," making you more resistant to the coming future.
- "Healing yourself to help heal the world."
- We live in a machine designed to get us to neglect what is important about life.
- Visualize the back of your heart; you don't want to die; you feel at this moment so empty and hopeless; this too shall pass.
- When these thoughts start to happen, you need to try to stop them immediately.
- Carefully, we will hold you until you can stand on your own. You are never alone.
- Reward yourself and write down good thoughts and feelings, such as your favorite food, music, videos, etc.
- Burn off those ways and things that no longer serve you.
- What is one thing I can change today — meditate on that, and you will get an answer.
- The revelation of your triumph but the depth of your despair is not nothing.
- Understand the tool of your mind and its proper role and purpose.
- We now limit our experiences by living through social media instead of being explorers, killing our tribe. It's a marketing tool, and that is it: take your power back.
- Our rationalism has stopped us from understanding.
- It's the ego that is thinking and driving the ship. Feel the depth of life's luminosity, what you might be capable of, and the different levels of consciousness that could be obtained or lost within you. It's your decision.
- Cruelty exists in every part of the world and breeds and multiplies like a virus among us. Feed it through separation, division, judgmental tactics, or go back to love at every moment. You will carry what you spew, whether it is good or bad.

- Being a kid is lonely. Your childhood wounding can't be rewritten, but you can redesign your life and genetics and reword what you say to yourself.
- Safety is essential for all humans. Give it, be it, take it, require it, hold it, and always offer it.
- All addictions are very hard energies. This must be healed for a complete experience. Hold space for struggling people, as they are your fellow brothers and sisters.
- I can tell friends that I am often suicidal because I maintain this sunny disposition to hide what I am going through. I am coping with the effects of losing my own will to live. Let the tribe in so they can hold you when you can't hold yourself.
- Suicidal ideation can become a silent obsession and addiction that you feel you have control over, but you do not; it has you just like any other addiction. Stop the wheel of looping these thoughts and words in your space and replace them with kindness for yourself.
- Some are looking and wanting permission to leave. We pray for you to stay.
- Bullying and suicide for teens are brutal. If you are looking for a cause, this one needs your help to stand and protect the children. Your soul will thank you.
- We need to start teaching social fitness to get out of overcoming fears.
- I agonize with the thought of death as it feels like it would be a relief or a welcome friend at times, but there is more for your eyes to see, your heart to feel, and your ears to hear.
- Find the light again, go through the gradient layers of grey matter and shadows, and take control of your light and soul.
- Keep the body and mind light, get out, and MOVE!

- Be ethical in all words. There are fragile humans on this Planet Earth.
- There is no good or bad, only creation.
- Grief has a role. It's the feeling that something is missing. A brief amount of grief is normal, but you need to do what you can to pull yourself out to the other side because the longer you hold onto it, the more spirits cannot communicate with your heart and your loved ones who have passed. They want to connect with you and continue to share their love.
- You are in a play inside your movie, with characters cast before you came to Planet Earth. See these roles, and it won't feel so heavy. Choose better storylines for each lesson!
- Recognize the small moments by making eye connections as much as possible. You might meet a soulmate just crossing a road — people are waiting to be recognized.
- We are made up of 50 trillion cells. Can you genuinely love all of them? The answer is yes, and then watch what happens!
- We should consider the concept of polarity, which involves looking at all sides. Often, humans focus on one side or the other, but we should recognize that everything is interconnected. This principle is not a modern concept; we must reconnect with our complete selves, not just our physical existence. Stepping away from social media is beneficial, as the images and content often lack spiritual depth and genuine adventure. Engaging with social media can lead to giving away our energy, abundance, and wealth to some celebrities who only provide a superficial representation of themselves. There will be a revolution, and humans will walk away once they realize it's making them sick and bored of its single dimension.
- Life is a yo-yo; when you let it go, it releases.

The Dark Energy: A Re-Education

Meditation. Start the Foundational Meditation for the Day for at least 15 minutes.

Gina Cavalier (Author-artist) and Dave King's (Singer-songwriter of the band Flogging Molly) wedding day in Las Vegas, Nevada, 10/24/98 (Wiki, n.d.)

Dave King, My Ex-Husband, and the Profound Lessons

I sketched a portrait of my ex-husband, Dave King, the lead singer of Flogging Molly. In my first book, *Surviving Suicidal Ideation*, I chronicled our relationship, depicting how we were brought together as soulmates to support each other's personal growth. Our intense connection was a significant part of my identity, and when we parted ways, I struggled as I needed to find my voice and establish my individuality. When I first met him, he hadn't even formed Flogging Molly yet; he was playing guitar and singing for booze in The Dave King band. Despite the challenges, I'm now grateful for the experiences that have significantly contributed to my spiritual growth. Even though our physical connection has changed, our spiritual bond remains strong. I often feel his presence in my dreams, where we share a cup of tea, hold hands, and have heartfelt conversations many years later. This place has no negativity, just two old souls saying, "Hello." I plan to delve deeper into these soulmate connections in the following text. Dave's challenging upbringing in Dublin, Ireland, where he grew up in poverty and lost his father at a young age, has influenced his spirituality and is reflected in his lyrics. I witnessed his emotions and struggles manifested in his art when I sat with him as he created his first four albums. I cried with him; I held him as he processed his emotions. He used to say, "I let an angel clip my wings." I was, and I knew it, spiritually an integral part of those creations, and I believe there has been a distinct change in his work since we've been separated, as the energy has shifted (although he would never admit it). If you are a sleeping spirit here on Earth, you will only see how you created a masterful work, but it's an orchestra of those around you: you, the instruments, and the spiritual realm creating those works. It is never a singular act, much like this handbook for the living.

Overall, his experiences have shaped his profound connection to the world of energy, which provided insight into the effects of dark or sorrowful energies and created his masterful music and lyrics. He wrote and recorded his first four albums when we were together. It was the first time I watched poetry and music come together. He would write, create, run into my room, and play me what he wrote. We sang, danced, laughed, and loved during those times. We slept holding hands for the first six years of our relationship. One day, he stopped holding my hand. Our union had been cut, and I would lose my best friend, and then he was gone. My entire being is grateful to have been part of our union and creating experiences and music together with spirit (I believe it was his best work when we were together because we were in this union and the energy of creation we brought in as a unit). However, I am so thrilled that I could get out of that vibration so I could soar into new heights of energy, and now I create my purposeful work to put out into the world. I know he cannot communicate with me, but he could be proud of my work, just as I was of him. All was not lost but fully gained, which was hard to see at the beginning of the split. Thank you, Dave. I'll see you in the next round of life; I am sure of that because "we all go the same way home," which was one of his lyrics. I genuinely believe that when we pass, we all get home.

It's natural to feel still a connection with someone who is no longer a part of your life. It can be somewhat healthy if you do not fixate on them or hope they will complete you. Sending a loving thought or a mental embrace to those individuals with whom you once shared moments of intimacy, laughter, and connection can be a way of acknowledging and respecting the journey you've been on. Although it may be challenging, particularly after experiencing betrayal, you may eventually perceive the situation differently. You may understand that it was a necessary part of your growth, helping you establish more robust and more empowering boundaries for yourself.

Nobody can tell you who and when to love. Even those who seemingly don't want anything to do with you in spirit will appreciate your loving thoughts. I have a long list of notable people with whom I still hold a little love, but I no longer talk, and I think that is just fine!

This picture represents my ex-husband, Dave King, creation with the shadows as I watched.

Archangel Helel (later humans named him Lucifer) and Archangel Michael. As indicated above, these gods, entities, and angels were partially born from humankind's needs and desires for them. Archangel Michael and Archangel Helel are twin flames (which will be detailed in soul contracts). But you need to know if they shared a part of the same soul. To give you an idea, it would be about 10% or sometimes more if that is what the souls choose. They were also considered twin brothers, as all archangels are born from the same cloth.

A Devil Was Made. At the time when Adam and Eve had more consciousness, everything was about love and abundance, and the source knew that humans needed to have lessons to grow as spirits; again, what would be the point if we were all just sitting around gardening? Archangel Helel knew there needed to be a representative and guide for this role. He was terrified, but he decided to take it because he did not want his brothers or sisters to have to endure what this meant, and a part of him was curious about the humans. He would sit and watch them experience the emotions that he wanted to experience. He seemed to be the only one that felt this way, and so it was. He was torn from the soul of Archangel Michael and brought from the universal cosmos to Earth in 3D, where the dark sediment of the Earth was created. This is very different from the darkness represented in the outermost universe. The Earthbound darkness is where you find the things that make your head shake, cry, and become shocked. Humans gave Archangel Helel the name of Lucifer. He was not kicked out of being an angel; that would have never happened. He thought he might return to his family one day when humans would eventually have learned their lessons. He has moments of remembering his family, and he cries and wants to go home. At those moments, he remembers the love, and he still wants it, but it has been so long that he has fewer moments of remembering who he originally was, which was an Archangel. These lower sediments or frequencies can seep into one's energy and almost bury one's soul in coal or an oil-like substance, making it hard to find and expose the light again. The only way Archangel Helel will get liberated is if all of humankind falls in love with each other and stops the divisions and hatred of one another. Until then, more illnesses, poor mental health, and wars will continue. But we are making headway right now, in fact, by being able to publish books like this one. Again, we will repeat that the more the individual heals, the more the world heals. Isn't it interesting how his name spells Hell? There is no physical hell except for what humans create on Earth. This is something that I knew as a child because of the terrible things that happen on this Planet; I knew there couldn't be another place with so much discord. Each person can make a massive change for the whole world; each soul is essential. If we can help as many people as possible return to love, this world would be completely different.

Wars were created by humanity, not the light nor the dark. It's hard to swallow this and see that as a collective, we not only made the most terrible things in the world but also maintained them. The cycle of righteousness, revenge, contempt, and ownership of lands that they could never or will never "actually own" is a falsehood that has been sold to humans. This keeps humanity stuck and trickles down like a poisoned river into our children, plants, animals, and oceans. However, what you do here and now is the most important and singular act of love for the Planet. As you do this work, not only will you care for your soul, but it will also spill out to all living energy around you. You will get more transparent on how powerful as an individual you are, and you will find a path that, when you do pass into the spiritual realm, you will be proud of the time and dedication you spent here as a "soul spark."

Just as there is a force that guides us toward life and light, there is also a force that guides us toward dark and death.

These forces can be personified, and often, they are because they are agrological in nature. Think about how many people have contemplated the source of all life across human history — billions of people. It is not benign. It's not meaningless; all that energy creates what is called an egregore, a collective thought form produced by the energies of humanity. With ritual and regular feeding of that thought form, it becomes alive. If fed specific energies, it can become spiritually activated and grow into what we call a God. The same can be said for the Darkness. Think about how many people across the span of human existence have contemplated the source of all darkness and fed energy into that, and it created an egregore. What you consider to be a traditional God of your bible exists because these beings have been brought into existence. Satan of our Bible has also been brought into existence. Are these beings the highest forms of spiritual existence and authority? No, because they originated on Earth, they are fundamentally Earth-based beings with compelling cosmic connections, but remember, the true source of all light and the true source of all darkness are **NOT AT ODDS WITH ONE ANOTHER.**

Why is this important to know? Because most of us fear the darkness in the world that is in and around us. We also create darkness when we think we stand up for the light. We are made up of both, and if we try to cleanse ourselves of every drop of darkness, we will be on a futile pursuit. We must also learn to dance with it beautifully and elegantly. Learning this brought me actual peace. The visions of darkness brought a lot of fear into my life. The dark knows how to show you those images that will keep you terrified and stuck. They seem so real, but they are mostly just visions or pictures. You are the one with a body, and you are the one with all the power. This is malignant energy thrown on you; as you run your energy, it cannot vibrate with you similarly. You will be liberated as you learn to walk with all the world's energies.

Don't Fear the Darkness (A true liberation story)

Having a physical body makes you more substantial than any other worldly energy. When you know that and fully embrace this knowingness, you will instantly be more potent against the things you fear, as they are much more limited to you. The darkest energies can only throw you a scary image (and I agree some of them are terrifying), but they are not here in the physical; you are! Some dark energies could harness energy to move an object or appear physically, but it takes so much energy for that moment that they are entirely depleted. It's like a battery that quickly gets killed. You are stronger!

I have seen energy, ghosts, angels, and entities since birth, which was terrifying. I learned a lot about life through movies of the times, and as a small child of seven, I watched movies with demons and exorcisms. I saw them more as documentaries because I had seen many of the same things. I would try and share them with my mother, and she would tell me, "You're possessed." I would think this could be true, so when I went to sleep at night, my "Night Terrors" would get activated, and I would journey through what felt like hell. In Spirit, I was traveling through the dark energies, and they know how to show you images that terrify you, all to keep you low and stuck. How did I know at that young age that I was the powerful one, holding all the cards because I had a body and could act? I could make things happen within this beautiful ecosystem of physical LOVE.

Archangel Helel embarks on leaving the Angels to become the dark representation of humanity.

Love Can Liberate a Demon

One night in my thirties, I had a full-blown night terror in my room. It happened in real time, and I had never had something so lifelike.

I was in bed. I felt physically paralyzed and could not move. My body was stiff from head to toe, and I could only move my eyes. There was a demon in my room, and it looked very similar to the demons in the movie *Constantine*. It appeared to me in this way because I worked on the Internet marketing campaign for that film, and I had a visceral response to seeing the demons in this film. I was like, "That is too close to home." Funny enough, I met the script screenwriter in a small bar in Donegal, Ireland, when I visited my family for a vacation. I asked him how he knew so much about the light and the dark, and he was a total atheist and didn't believe in anything. I said, *"Yeah, but your Spirit does, and it has seen some things!"*

This demon did not look healthy and looked like it was dying. It had stringy limbs and sores. I captured its eyes, which were human and kind; I saw its deep sadness and struggle. I usually fought hard in my room during these visits, like in a war, calling in my tools and my light angels and guides—a battle that would last what felt like hours, and I would awaken exhausted from the night's events.

I would try something different this time. First, I ran the tools that you have been taught here on myself. Then, I hooked up the demon to Source and started praying for him and running the tools on him. I put him in a bright ball of light and imagined dumping as much love into his vessel as possible. It felt a little violent energetically at times; it was scary, too, but I persisted — light, love, more light, more love. I thought, *"What if that was my child, and he was stuck? Wouldn't I want to heal him?"*

I started to see him shift and mutate through various avatars. Then the darkness fell away, and I could see the boy underneath. He was very young and looked about 17 years old, but he was now fresh-faced, with bright blue eyes, freckles, and glowing white skin. He smiled at me as tears fell down his cheek. I heard in my knowingness, *"You liberated me with your love like a mother would."* His soul sent me a blessing, and he vanished. This stuck with me and is partly why my company has the word "Liberated" ingrained into the energy. I knew then that even the darkness wants love. That it is not separated, and that is where we are getting a lot of things wrong. Everything and everyone can benefit from love. That is how you change the world, yourself, your family, and your friends.

Reminder: Just because love is a great healer does not mean we are doormats and should let people take us over. We need boundaries and to put ourselves first. That is just being strong in how you run your life. With these tools and lessons, that is what you are learning. We call this *"Being in your seniority."* You can manifest and create the world you want when you get here.

Week 3. Day 5 – Earth Angels/Our Guide Sue-Ellen/The Liberated Healer Zipper Meditation

Meditation. Start the Foundational Meditation for the Day for at least 30 minutes.

This is one of my favorite subjects because my guides have been excellent to get to know and have helped me feel supported in so many ways. I want to introduce you to Sue-Ellen, one of my guides for this book, pictured here in an image I channeled of how she looks.

My Earth Angel/Spirit Guide, Sue-Ellen, suffered from Suicidal Ideation when she lived on Planet Earth.

Earth Angels. Sue-Ellen says you can say her name with a southern twang. She is here to help those who are depressed or suicidal and is empathic because this is her story when she is here on the planet. In the channel, you will hear where the book title came from! Earth Angels are just what they sound like. They decided to go to Earth to help humanity and were previously just angels. The issue for Sue-Ellen and myself (I am also an Earth Angel) is that we are so sensitive and willing to give so much that we have nothing left for ourselves. I am lucky that I was able to turn this around, but it is also the reason that in some of my past lives, I have committed suicide. Sue-Ellen almost always killed herself when she was a human. It breaks her heart to see humanity and its impact on each other, animals, and the planet. She is getting healing from this book, and she can be with you, too, if you call her name three times and ask for her assistance.

Channeled Message from Sue-Ellen:
"I am honored to be a part of this team. I can't say that I am the exclusive guide for this co-creation. I can say this is my story that you are telling, and I have been incarnated to live it multiple times, so you and I are corded in the best ways I will not extract from you or distract you. I will be here mainly in a heap with streams of tears running down my face. I thank you if I were to have a face and tears because you are telling my story and preventing me from reliving it again. Thank you for this. I am highly relatable, and you will feel me. Do you feel me now? I hope you feel me now because we are partnered this way, and I am not here walking the planet. I have had to take a sabbatical from the Planet Walking. Even though I love Planet Walking. Oh boy, do I love it, but it is difficult because it is heavy and my heart is always problematic; congenitally so, in each birth, I have chosen a problematic heart, and then the addition of the difficulties and the intensities and the feelings that I have that are so

big, so enormous and so similar in fact to yours. We have a soft spot for every creature, human, and more than human that might need our support and assistance, so we dive right in — don't we? We will give not just the shirt off our backs but the hair off our heads, the skin off our bodies, and all the things — sacrifice after sacrifice. Please include the tendency to sacrifice ourselves. It is a piece of why I need it to be illuminated. Suppose I agree to return and come back with the powerful healing that I have and hold, that I happily distribute and disseminate everywhere it is needed, but for now. In that case, I will stay here and work with you whenever you need me, and yes, my name is Sue-Ellen, and I am here, I am here."

Her essence is so beautiful, and she is tucked in the loop of what this book is meant to free people from. She does not want to be here because it is so heavy, and she wants to be here and on Planet Walk. She supports us and reminds us how to heal and get through it. Thank you, Sue-Ellen, for being with us.

The Liberated Healer's "Zipper Energy"

In this meditation, you will "zip" yourself up into a bubble of light energy around your body and auric field in the morning and evening. You will then "unzip" to let the stagnant energy out and call in new energy for the night.

You do not need any prior meditation experience. The routine will be created by simply engaging your body and mind through acting, reading, or speaking these instructions. In other words, you cannot do this incorrectly. Let go of any ideas of doing it perfectly, doing it for the right amount of time, or anything that might create a false sense of effort. The spirit knows what to do if you lose your place. It is your dutiful partner. We suggest the first few times, you be in a quiet space so you can see, hear, or feel the subtle shifts. Again, if you cannot, that is perfectly fine. The healing work is still happening.

Once familiar with the process, you can do it anywhere at any time that you might need an energetic bump of protection and grounding. Even if you cannot move, you will still benefit from imagining the process.

Zipping In (Morning)

1. Upon waking, we need to shake off the stagnant energy from the night. Begin by standing up and gently moving your neck and shoulders. Shake your arms and your hands, then your hips and legs at a good pace. Root to the Earth below you and crunch your toes. If it feels good, bend your hips and swing your body from side to side while reaching for the floor. Note: Most animals do their version of this practice upon waking. They will shake off the energy, often starting at their heads and down through their tails or feet. We have lost this instinct and practice in our modern world, but energy is vital.
2. Coming back to your bed or a seat in the room, sit in a comfortable position. If possible, do not cross your arms or legs so as not to stop the flow of energy through bent extremities.
3. With closed eyes (or a soft gaze in front of you), turn the sides of your mouth up slightly (which in dialectical behavioral therapy is called a "half smile"). If this action feels forced, you can imagine doing so, allowing the healing energy of smiling to wash over you.
4. Say out loud or in your head, "Hello," repeating the word as many times as feels good to you. This does three things:
    - It brings you into the here and the now into the present time.
    - Connects your mind, body, and spirit.

- Alerts any guides or angels you have around you that you are ready to work.

5. Stretch your arms over your head and notice where the edges of your fingertips are. This is the top edge of the auric field you are working on. Keep your arms straight, and slowly circle the entire energy field around you like a giant bubble, ending with your hands down near your seat.
6. With your feet on the ground, imagine you are bringing energy from the Earth up through the center of your feet into your calves, knees, thighs, hips, and torso. This will ground you while cleaning out any stuck energy.
7. Focus now just above your head and imagine a vibrant rainbow of colors that grows into the bubble you created with your arms. There are no muted colors here — instead, the energy of glorious red, orange, yellow, green, blue, and purple.
8. Notice any areas of your body or energy field that feel stuck, tense, or need attention. Send this rainbow of energy to that location in your body or mind.
9. Now, imagine the power of golden sunlight growing just over your head and on the back of your neck.
    - You can say to yourself or aloud: "I call back my life force energy and highest vibration of light."
    - Imagine the golden light falling over you like a shower of energy.
    - Stay here in this flow of light as long as needed. Once you feel energized and ready, move to the final step.
10. Reach your arms straight out again above your head and grasp onto a giant imaginary zipper. Imagine zipping up the bubble around you with your new, glorious energy.
11. Move throughout the rest of your day with this newfound energetic protection.

Zipping Out (Evening)

Your energy can stagnate despite being zipped up and protected all day. Return to this practice just before lying down to sleep.

1. Connecting with your body, shake from head to toe — this time to release tension carried throughout the day.
    - Coming back to your bed or a seat in the room, sit in a comfortable position (or lie down if you want to use this as a practice to induce sleep).
    - Reach your arms straight out again above your head, reaching with your fingers for a giant zipper. Pull it open — imagine unzipping the entire bubble around you and letting out your day's energy.
    - With closed eyes (or a soft gaze in front of you), turn the sides of your mouth up slightly in a half smile.
    - Say out loud or in your head, "Goodnight," which:
        - It brings you into the here and the now into the present time.
        - Connects your mind, body, and spirit.
        - Alerts any guides or angels you have around you that you are ready for rest.
    - Stretch your arms straight up over your head and circle your energy bubble. Let fresh energy from the Earth flow throughout your torso.
    - Bring back your rainbow of colors into the bubble you created with your arms.
    - Notice any areas of your body or energy field that feel stuck, tense, or need attention. Send this rainbow of energy to that location in your body or mind.
    - Imagine the warm glow of the moon growing just over your head and on the back of your neck.
        - You can say to yourself, "I invite rest and peace."
        - Stay here in this glow of the moonlight as long as needed.

- Follow your breath and invite the comfort of rest and sleep.

This is an image of a Seraphim Angel; they are of the highest order above Archangels and have four faces (one that faces North, South, East, and West).

Week 3. Day 6 – Angels, Guides, Ascended Masters – Re-Education

Meditation. We can choose which meditation you want, but at least do The Liberated Healer's Zipper Energy Meditation or the Grounding Meditation.

The book has a soul and an energy. It is a collection of pure information intended to help humanity have a spiritual soul and connection to the universe. All those who interact with it, promote it, use it, fund it, and more are a part of this expression. The book has an energy that it carries and is very healing. The energy is set to hold space for you in protection as much as possible (as much as you will let in). There is so much more to learn, and you are never alone. Thank you for doing the work; as each human raises their frequency and gets re-educated, it lifts the Planet 100-fold! You are not just helping yourself but every living thing around you!

You are working with your Guides/Clear Information. Only you know how to communicate with your guides, so make it personal. Here are some words I recommend putting out into the universe.

- Please ensure that I serve only the highest vibrational match and bring in only those of similar vibrations.
- Please help me find time in my day to connect to spirit meaningfully.
- Please help me develop clear signs, so I know it is you. Some things resonate with me (for example, butterflies, numbers, flowers, or songs).
- I want to feel your presence by clear words or visions downloaded.
- What are my next steps? Please show me some guidance through colors or symbols.
- Please include humor in my receiving.

The Guides & Angels. If you are reading this and working on the program, the guides supporting this work are also part of your spiritual team. Even when you move on from this energy, you will take it as part of what you have learned, and this information can be called upon at any time. You might fall back into old patterns during healing and stop working on this effort. It's all at your pace and what you decide; when you are ready to pick it back up, it's right there at your beck and call. All spirit loves you and will jump in when you are ready. It's a nice feeling to know that there is an entire group of angels, guides, ascended masters, and ancestors who are there to help pull up your bootstraps when you need them. The reality is we are never alone, which can be a good feeling.

Your Primary Guides. Everyone is born with two guides who stay with them their entire lives. The first is a guardian angel, and the other is a guide who helps you stay on track and on your path. However, it can be of assistance to you.

Angels and Gods. The angels and the Gods humans have given rise to are brought consciously and continue to be brought into existence as intermediaries; they are personifications of the stars and celestial phenomena we experience within the cosmic universe. To call upon the power of a star, you must have a means, a way of accessing it; thus, a God is brought into existence that represents the power of that desired star. God is the personification of this because God is somewhat humanlike. It can be interacted with because God can be named, summoned, and communicated with. It acts as a way for the mortal/human to be entangled with and draw upon the powers of the divine realm to create all types of things. These spiritual practices and procedures were used to build Western and Eastern civilization.

Mediumship – How does it work?

The vessel or human goes into a trance-like state, the spirit guide steps into their energy or auric field, and they can set up their communication system. In this process, they raise their frequency and vibration to match each other, and in doing so, usually, the human will get healing because all low vibrational energy will fall off.

Baby Beings

Our agreement to collaborate often involves the creation and nurturing of new life. The soul begins to form in the womb around six weeks into the development of the body. At times, as the body develops, there may be physical challenges, and the soul can observe what life would be like in that body. It then has the choice to continue in that body or to seek another. This represents the exercise of free will. If the soul accepts the circumstances of its birth, even if it entails physical difficulties, it can embrace the experience as an opportunity for growth and learning. Ultimately, it's a process driven by love and transformation, and it's truly a beautiful journey. The soul is everlasting so if they are meant to be birthed in this timeline by a particular family of souls it will make sure it comes through, so know they are always with you.

Guides:

This is a big topic and can be very confusing, so we will focus only on what you need to know for this work. If they pique your interest, we will list many resources in the back section so you can dive in and learn more.

Light a candle, incense, or any other ritual to let the guides know you are ready to communicate.

- **Ancestor** – Ancestors are our blood relatives who have passed away from this life or a past life in our soul family. They provide us with guidance and wisdom from their experiences or our shared experiences, and they want to remind us of a lesson we learned or need to learn.
- **Ancestor Guides** – A beloved loved one who is no longer physically on the Planet.
- **Angels** – Angels are powerful beings who can provide guidance and protection. You can communicate with

them and research them and their talents to see which ones might best help you with your specific needs. They like to send signs, and if you have something specific you would like to be shown, say a particular sequence of numbers, an animal, a bird, or a butterfly, let them know, and they will try to meet you where you can receive the best. They do not hold human emotion; they are only pure love. They see us struggle and will go into overdrive to help lift us with positive vibrations. They will also try to align us with other souls we are meant to work with, which often feels like a serendipitous meeting.

- **Animals** – Animal spirit guides provide us with guidance and support. To communicate with them, pay attention to the animals you encounter and their behavior, and look up their symbolic meanings. Animals are like angels in that they are only pure love. Even if they were to attack a human, that would be just for survival, but they only knew love in their energy. They are hyper-aware of our energy. They can sense danger at least in a 2-mile radius for them and us. If we build trust with animals or birds, they will always send us loving support. We must, in turn, try to help these lovely creatures worldwide as they have been abused, used, and killed in horrific conditions. Humanity is sick in this category, and if we ever want to live in a utopia for all, we must change the way we engage with our animals.
- **Archangels – Archangels are mighty angels who can protect and guide us.** To communicate with them, invoke their names, and ask for their help and guidance. There are female and male archangels. Although there are male and female archangels, it has more to do with the energy than the actual gender. Still, because for such a long time, these angels have been not only named with names that are masculine or feminine and prayed upon, or visualized

as such, they appear to us the way we want to see them and how they want to be represented as it helps us to understand their place in the universe. Although the art is beautiful and represents them, they are just an enormous, bright, soul-looking energy. They are not separate from us but reflect our highest capacity to love and be loved. For example, Archangel Michael is mainly seen in a suit of arms with an almighty sword of Truth.

Male Archangels

- Michael – Protector and the Leader of the Army of God
- Gabriel – Messenger of God, Reveals Prophecies and News
- Raphael – Healer and Guide, Restores Health and Wellness
- Uriel – Angel of Wisdom, Brings Warnings and Insights
- Raguel – Angel of Harmony, Friend of God Held with Conflicts
- Remiel – Angel of Hope, Guides Souls after Death, Comfort and Divine Visions
- Sariel/Azreal – Angel of Death, Guides Souls to the Afterlife
- Jerahmeel (or Jeremiel) – Mercy of God and Serves Humanity, Presence, Visions, and Dreams
- Metatron – Angel of Life, Tree of Life, and the Keeper of Scribes. (Not everyone agrees that this being is an Archangel, but I have worked with him for many years and find he is now an archangel.)

Female Archangels. They are the existential essence of the above male Archangels, the inner, energetic potential, and creativity to thrust one's need into existence, such as "grace." This is when they come in to balance the duality of the two energies needed in all things — light/dark and masculine/feminine. Their names are self-explanatory to what they address.

- Faith
- Virtue
- Hope
- Purity
- Victory
- Grace
- Charity
- Mercy
- Freedom
- Harmony
- Patience
- Serenity
- Strength
- Constance
- Radiant
- Joy

- **Ascended Masters** – Ascended masters are highly evolved spiritual beings who can provide guidance and wisdom. Communicate with them, meditate on their image or name, and ask for their help and advice. Here are just a few of these fantastic beings: Afra, Anandamayi Ma, Babaji, Gautama Buddha, Christ Jesus, Confucius, Djwhal Khul, El Morya, Elijah, Ganesha, God Mercury, Hathor, Hermes Trimegistus, Hilarion, Krishna, Kuthumi, Lady Nada, Lady Portia, Lahiri Mahasaya, Lanto, Maha Chohan, Maitreya, Mary Magdalene, Meher Baba, Melchizedek, Merlin, Milarepa, Mother Mary, Maitreya, Sai Baba, Sanat Kumara, St. Germain, Qyan-yin, Ramtha, Rowena, St. Teresa of Avila, Yogananda, Yukteswar, and Zoroaster.
- **Ascension Guides** – They are always trying to get your attention to raise the frequency, continue to learn, and

stay on track with your life's purpose. They step forward when you start doing deep healing work.

- **Counsels/Community Groups Guides with one or more voices –** We are seeing this increasingly, especially with channels that collectively share important information with the world. There are too many to list, but we know them as you seek information.
- **Earth Angels –** Angels that were in the celestial realm but have decided to lose their wings to come to Earth to help humanity. They are here, living amongst us, and waiting to come down. They usually have complex lives when they are here. I am an Earth Angel, which explains why I gave all of myself for so long that I almost expired until I did this work. They often kill themselves as the Earth's energy is dense, and the pain they feel when they see the horrors of the world can take them down.
- **Elementals –** Elementals are spirits that represent the four elements (earth, air, fire, and water). They can help us connect with the natural world and guide us on our spiritual path. To communicate with them, spend time in nature and focus on the element you wish to connect with. They hold the spiritual universal consciousness.
- **Gatekeeper Guides –** They guard your soul records (Akashic religion records). They connect you with the memories and wound healing at the right time to bring the healing, advancement, wisdom, and knowledge of your soul's memories into your current experience without overwhelming them. Gatekeeper guides also work to allow or block entities depending on what is for your highest and greatest good.
- **Gods and Goddesses/Deities –** These are powerful energies that help you, in many cases, to reach the goals that you have set out. Research the ones that you are drawn to that you want to build a relationship with.

Here are some listed. There are many more and in many different cultures. There are too many to list, but they are easy to find in a search. Here are just some to pique your interest.

- **African – Female:** Aja, Aje, Ayao, Egungun-Oya, Mawu, Nana Buluku, Oba, Odudua, Olokun, Oshun, Oya, Yemaja. **Male:** Aganju, Babalu-Aye, Erinle, Eshu, Kokou, Obatala, Oduduwa, Ogun, Olokun, Olorun, Oshosh, Shango.
- **Chinese:** Yudi, Doumu, Pangu, Xiwangmu, Yanwang, Yinanggong, Fuxi, Nuwa, Shennong, Wudi, Huangdo, Heidi, Cangdi, Baidi.
- **Greek – Male:** Achilles, Apollo, Ares, Theseus, Odysseus, Perseus, Jason, Bellerpohon, Orpheus, Cadmus, Hector, Paris, Oedipus, Dionysus, Hermes, Hephaestus, Poseidon, and Zeus. **Female:** Artemis, Athena, Aphrodite, Demeter, Hera.
- **Hindu:** Brahma, Hanuman, Shiva, Ganesha, Buddhahood, Vishnu, Kamadeva, Krishan, Durga, Rama, Pavali, and Lakshmi.
- **Irish – Male:** Dagda, Nuada, Bres, Aoi, Lugh, Ogma, Bile, Aengus, Dian Cecht, Luchtaine, Goibniu, Creiohne Oshosh Danu, Boann, Banbha, Brigid, Ernmas, Aine, Morrigan, Macha, Glioohna, Fand.
- **Norsk:** Thor, Ullr, Yggdrasil, Freya, Odin, Frigg, Balder, Loki, Njordr, Hel, Skadi.

- **Healer Guides** – They help to elevate our physical, emotional, and mental well-being.
- **Helper Guides** – They help you with your goals, bringing in your soulmates and twin flames.
- **Joy Guides** – They bring lighthearted energy to you when you need it.
- **Karmic Guides** – They are here to help us navigate personal and collective karma so that we can resolve it,

step off the wheel of karma, and experience new levels of love and blessings through dharma.

- **Life Guides** – Managers of your spirit guide team. These guides are with you from birth to death and work to manage and coordinate all the other spirit guides, angels, and teacher guides assisting you at any given time. These guides include Helper, Healing, Way-Shower, Past Life, Financial, Health, Creativity, Protection, Astral, Librarians, Healers, Warriors, Protectors, and Joy.
- **Light Beings** – They have never incarnated on Planet Earth and bring us light.
- **Runner Guides** – They help with daily things you need assistance with, like parking. They can go ahead and scope things out for you.
- **Spirit Animals** – Spirit animals appear in our dreams or meditations to provide guidance and support. To communicate with them, focus on the animals that appear in your dreams or meditations and research their symbolic meanings. Here are a few examples: Bears, Eagles, Dolphins, Whales, Elephants, Gorillas, Jaguar, Rhino, Giraffe, Deer, Buffalo, Horse, Tiger, Dolphin, Bees, Spider, Snakes, Beaver, Fox, Wolf, Ant, Turkey, Rabbit, Armadillo, Skunk, Dog, Otter, Lizard, Weasel, Badger, Turtle, Dragonfly, Boar, Frog, Moose, Blue Heron, Hawk, Elk, Owl, Bat, Coyote, Alligator, Crow, Lynx, Hummingbird, Mouse, Butterfly, Swan, Sea Lion, and Pelican.
- **Star Beings** – Star beings are extraterrestrial beings who can provide us with guidance and wisdom. Communicate with them, meditate on the stars or the cosmos, and ask for their help and advice. Many people here who are deep into spirituality came from the stars, which means they had lives outside of Earth. They can also have difficulty living on Earth in its heavy form, where they are used to the light and fluffy energy.

- **Teacher Guides** – Appear to teach you and guide you along your path. They will appear in different forms depending on your lessons and objectives. They guide dreams and meditation and leave clues and signs for you, if needed, before moving on. They pay attention to the cycles in our lives and some challenges that stop us from learning and help us.
- **Timing Guides** – *Oversee synchronicity in your life. They will help you be in the right place at the right time, meet critical people on your path, and align with new opportunities at a divine time.*

A Story about Timing Guides. Lately, I received channeled messages suggesting I would reunite with someone from my eternal soul family. This person and I are interconnected on a deep level and usually go through life cycles together. We had both been working on ourselves to reach a point where we could meet again as we reflected on each other's journeys. Periodically, I received updates about this individual. He had established a successful life for himself, but there were some significant areas where he felt unfulfilled, including deep love, passion, and creativity. Despite this, he had a fulfilling life with a large family, many friends, a successful career, and respect in his community. He was moving forward, but this aspect of his life seemed stagnant. As he approached age 60, he began expressing his desires and progressing towards manifesting these elements through spiritual work.

In contrast, I had abundant passion, creativity, and deep love in various aspects of my life, but I lacked stability regarding family, friends, and work. I was actively working on these areas to create the life I envisioned. At the age of mid-50s, I was also doing spiritual work.

Surprisingly, I received an invitation in my email for an event in a location where I wanted to spend more time and relocate. I made the spontaneous decision to attend. As soon as I arrived at the event, I made eye contact with him – he was the first person I spoke to. Initially, I only felt a strange "knowing" about him but nothing extraordinary until he approached me later in the evening, and we connected deeply. It felt like an electric current surged through my body like I had found my long-lost best friend. He has been a valuable presence in my life, providing encouragement, support, love, and much more. Curious about the timing of our meeting, I asked my guides why they had previously indicated that this person wouldn't enter my life for another seven months. They responded, "Yes, but you were doing so much work and needed each other. If we had told you the exact timing, you would have been looking out for it. Isn't it better this way?" They knew the best timing for us and would provide what we needed, especially if we were attentive and committed to our personal growth.

How Do They Communicate with Us?

- Intuition – Spirit guides can communicate with us through intuition, which provides a sense of inner knowing or a gut feeling about a situation.
- Dreams are one of the easiest ways our spirit guides communicate with us, offering guidance or messages through symbols or metaphors.
- Signs and symbols – Spirit guides use signs and symbols in the physical world, such as numbers, animals, or objects that hold significance to us.
- Physical sensations – Spirit guides can communicate through bodily sensations, such as a feeling of warmth or a tingling sensation.
- Telepathy – Spirit guides use telepathy to communicate, sending thoughts or messages to our minds.

- Through other people – Spirit guides can use others as messengers, providing guidance or messages through friends, family members, or strangers.

Week 3. Day 7 – Integration Day/Pendulum Work

This was a massive week. Please relax and integrate all the knowledge and lessons today, and we will be doing a fun exercise that doesn't overtax the brain too much. Take extra time today to have fun and realize activities like taking a hot bath, walking in nature, and more.

Item Needed: A pendulum or a small chain at least 5 inches long.

A Pendulum Sample or anything on a chain link that can move back and forth or side-by-side.

I agree that rosework can be a lot to learn, but it changes lives and has an entire ecosystem of learning that can move into advanced teaching. But sometimes you want something more leisurely, and we have many questions to ask in the next week, so here we will learn simple pendulum teachings. This neat tool will also help you channel in later times with practice.

My Pendulum Story. I have discovered that various things, including the human body, can serve as an energetic pendulum. People process energy and information differently; my body strongly responds to physical stimuli. When I engage in extensive healing work and clearing, I often experience a phenomenon where I begin to "burp." It's not a superpower I would have chosen for myself, but it's something that I've found challenging to transmute in other ways. It becomes uncomfortable if I don't allow myself to burp when the sensation arises. Therefore, I've learned to accept the need to burp for the sake of healing at times. During my quest for profound healing, I found meditation to be incredibly beneficial, particularly during my time spent with the Hindus. Their practices deeply resonate with me, and I've integrated them into my approach and work.

I vividly recall a moment during group meditation when I felt like I had transcended my physical form and was soaring among the stars and planets. I chose to visit Saturn, drawn to its mesmerizing rings and the pulsating energy they emitted. As I extended my hand, I felt the energies flow through my fingers and into my being. While experiencing this, my body involuntarily started to sway in circular motions, like a pendulum. This sensation was part of an energy-tuning process, aligning me with the Earth and the entirety of existence, allowing me to feel weightless and unseen. This same energy is also utilized when seeking to communicate with tools or objects, enabling active communication with any entity. It's a beautiful, playful, and gentle experience, offering a unique form of interaction. We are often encouraged to relinquish our sense of wonder and innocence from a young age. However, I embrace this sense of wonder and invite it into my life. We all have an enchanting rendezvous with the universe, and I intend to savor every moment. Thank you, universe!

Pendulum Foundation: Please remember the following instructions for practicing with a pendulum or chain. Find a quiet and private space with a closed door and allow yourself at least 15 minutes for your practice. If you start to feel tired, it's okay to stop; don't push yourself too hard. Using a pendulum requires focus, which can be draining.

Make sure to have a flat surface to balance your arm and hold the chain with your thumb and index finger. Practice watching the pendulum swing and notice how it changes in different positions. The feel of the pendulum will vary depending on its weight and design.

You can bring objects like crystals, feathers, or items with grounding energy to create a sacred environment. You can also get photos or other personal items that make the space unique.

As you start to feel the power of the pendulum, it might be exciting and a little intimidating if you're not used to experiencing energy shifts like this.

Assume Position: Place your arm on a flat surface and hold the pendulum, allowing it to swing about 2 inches above the surface. Please pay attention to any noticeable direction in which it swings, side to side or back and forth. You can experiment with it and observe how the pendulum reacts to subtle movements in your fingers. I've found that these micro-movements can influence the direction of the swing.

Start by having the pendulum feel your energy by opening your palm and letting it swing over your hand.

You can start by saying, *"Hello, Spirit and Guides. Thank you for today's interaction. Can you please give me an answer of yes?" It will move up and down like a head nod or in a* clock*wise circle.*

You can continue by saying, *"Hello, Spirit and Guides, thank you for today's interaction. Can you please show me an answer to No?" It will be side-by-side or in a* counterclock*wise circle.*

Clear the Start. Pendulum spiritual hygiene to clear the energy. You can dip in the water, under a full moon or sunlight, or use other clearing methods like sage or palo santo. Who do you want counsel from? You can ask your spirit guides or your higher self, the go-to team, for general questions. You can also ask questions from people who have passed, alive, or anyone. Just show gratitude and appreciation for anyone who comes in to offer help.

When you are comfortable communicating, we can start. Stop the motion by holding the item for a moment or leaning it on the surface; this signals to the spirit that you are done with the other lines of questions. If it feels that you are in rhythm and stable with your pendulum, you don't have to reprogram it again unless you think you need to later for better communication.

Start with easy questions to test it. Is my name ____________________ and see what you get. At times, the pendulum will go even faster or slower; that motion will give you a sense of how strong the answer is to your YES or NO. You can ask it to swing bigger if you want, as well. It's all about communication. You can also close your eyes if you are trying not to influence the outcome. Make sure your arm is supported.

Do I live on ______________________ street? Just test it a few times. We must be tuned to your awareness and the tools and energy that are working together.

When there is an answer for "I don't know, maybe, not now, or not determined," the tool will do a shimmy, vibrate, or wiggle. You can even ask, "Is that a maybe?" and then you will get an answer.

Go ahead and start asking some questions you are curious about. We will use this technique, or rosework, to find answers to these questions. Enjoy your new tool!

BEE & Hanuman – Week 4 – Your Soul Gifts and Themes and Life's Purpose

This week, the Bee is our Spirit Animal, and Hanuman, the Hindu God, is showing itself.

Cultivating a garden may start with small beginnings. However, the industrious bee still needs to enter and partake in the fruits of labor while contributing to its flourishing ecosystem through tireless work. Through unwavering effort and determination, all life within the garden is sustained. Bees play a crucial role in sustaining life, and as humanity becomes more conscious of this fact, we will come to recognize their significance. In our united effort, we will take steps to eliminate the harmful effects of 5G wireless technology, which threatens bees and, consequently, us. Hanuman is here to remind us that we hold unlimited power that lies unused within each human. We can become free from physical fatigue and illness if we harness this energy.

Week 4. Day 1 – Soul's Blueprint (Gifts)

Your Soul's Blueprint

Meditation. We can choose which meditation you want, but at least do The Liberated Healer's Zipper Energy Meditation or the Grounding Meditation.

You Choose This Experience to Grow. You are in a play inside your movie, with characters cast before you came to Planet Earth. See these roles, and it won't feel so heavy. Choose better storylines for each lesson! Understanding how each soul enters this physical existence as a divine being of light can be complex. The purpose of all living beings is to fulfill a goal. Take the example of an acorn — its sole objective is to grow into a mighty oak tree. Every aspect of its existence is dedicated to finding fertile soil, absorbing sunlight, and managing its water supply, all in the relentless pursuit of life despite its limited mobility.

Similarly, our original goal as human beings is to learn and grow, albeit with a different level of consciousness than our plant counterparts. We are here to gain profound insights into life through the lessons we experience. Our mission is not aimless; instead, it is to accumulate diverse life experiences based on our chosen themes. In doing so, we contribute to elevating the collective consciousness.

Furthermore, some souls may briefly enter this physical realm to guide others and facilitate their learning, resulting in a shorter lifespan for themselves. The following chapters will discuss this more, particularly about soul contracts.

Additionally, some souls enter this world to heal others, including their souls, their families, and the world. Often, they endure intense and challenging lessons in the initial stages of their lives due to taking on excessive burdens, only finding balance and stability later. This resonates deeply with my journey. Understanding why I had to endure such struggles has enabled me to create a brighter future for myself and to extend forgiveness to both me and others for their roles in my experiences.

For example, I wanted to have children in this life, but by the time I was 19, I had lost the ability to conceive from my tubal pregnancies. This always pained me as I wanted that experience and connection, but by uncovering my soul's blueprint, I understood why this was not my path for me earlier in life.

- First, I was told that I needed to learn how to mother myself in this lifetime.
- I had a past life where I was expected to have as many children as possible, and I had about 18 pregnancies. Which I thought was crazy because when digging into my personal history through DNA, I learned that my great-grandmother from Ireland had 18 children. I'm not saying that was my soul, but I wondered how that could be possible. When I was building this life, I felt like a baby-making machine in the past, and I wanted to avoid that in this life, so I did.

These things helped me see why some things I deemed horrifying might have been part of the original plan. My soul already knew the experience of children. I've learned some core lessons, such as how to mother myself, balance emotions, heal from most traumas, and create healthy boundaries in my life. If I wanted to experience a child, I could consider adoption in the future.

Your Soul's Blueprint. As human beings, we are the creators of our destinies. Before entering this world, we made conscious decisions about the kind of person we wanted to be, the family we wanted to be a part of, and the physical form we tried to inhabit. These decisions were made alongside a collective group, and the people we encounter in this life may be individuals we have crossed paths with numerous times before. There are certain souls with whom we share such a deep connection that we seem to reunite with them in different lifetimes, and our bond remains unbroken. Meeting these souls in the physical realm is a compelling and spiritual experience. Although I've only encountered this once so far, I've been told I will have the opportunity to experience it with other souls. Some refer to these deep connections as "twin flame souls," but it goes beyond that and requires a more in-depth explanation, which I plan to delve into in a future chapter.

Ultimately, we are all interconnected on a profound level. At the core of our being, we are driven by a desire to acquire knowledge and experience everything the universe offers. We already hold the vast universe within ourselves.

What does the blueprint look like? When you are ready to sit down and go into your meditation to go through and see what you feel is your soul's blueprint, please go to "rosework" to begin. Yes, it starts out looking just like a blueprint. There is a bright blue light around the being. There are some ingested core lessons from the past life you want to heal.

Rose/Pendulum work. Pull up a rose to get a yes or no answer to each item, or use your pendulum to get your answers today.

1. Pick the primary colors that will move through your body. For example, my primary color is green, and my secondary color is indigo.
    - **Yellow** – I have been here before. I am here to learn. I am here to unravel karma. I will stay on my path.
    - **Green** – I am here to feel. I feel it all. I see and touch me. I see and feel you. We are a community. We belong together. I am here to teach you about interpersonal communication.
    - **Blue** – I see, touch, feel, and KNOW. I know and must tell, share, show, and demonstrate my knowingness. I must lead you toward your knowingness.
    - **Indigo** – I am not me; I am part of you. I share, guide, and sacrifice for us. I remember.
    - **Orange** – I validate that what I see, touch, feel, hear, and taste is authentic, But I also notice that others have and can have other experiences. What is going on? What is that?
    - **Red** – To hear, see, touch, taste, and smell is to be authentic.
    - **Violet** – We are not separate, but all the same. I shine in the darkness, brief and luminous. I am aware from the first breath till last. I do not need to be here long. These are high vibrational beings that leave us sooner than later.

    What is your Primary Color?

    ____

2. See if you have any secondary colors by doing the same work.

   Secondary: Red, Yellow, Green, Orange, Blue, or Indigo

   What is your Secondary Color?

   ___

3. See what "Primary Gifts" you have come in with here:
   A. Energy Sensitive. B. Empathetic. C. Both Energy and Empathetic. D. Earth Sense

   What are your Primary Gifts?

   ___

4. What are your Secondary Gifts? Use the Rose or the Pendulum and review each item below to find the soul-specific "gifts" you have come into this life with. In this section, you will find many gifts. You might be surprised at what your gifts are, but figuring this out is usually very helpful to people to understand their life's purpose. For example, I have 16 out of the 33 below gifts.

What are your Secondary Gifts?

___

___

Dream Traveler – Person or entity that travels in their dream space to gain knowledge or to connect with other souls	**Dream Weaver** – Person or entity that possesses the ability to create and manipulate dreams	**Thoughtography** – Medium that can form images onto ectoplasm from the mind
Levitation is the suspension of an object or person off the ground without any visible form of support	**True Speak** – When we stop searching for spiritual truth as something that you can find, or as something that can be explained – we start to allow it to find us	**Materialization** – When our practice reinforces, bolsters, separates and inflates our ego
Astral Travel – Astral body has left their physical body and moved into another dimension	**Remote Viewing** – Process through which you can question whether the information is remote to the viewer or whether the process is entirely visual	**Entity Recognition/"real-time"** – An ability to recognize any entity in real-time like angels, guides, and more
Psychic Surgery – Unique form of healing that combines spiritual and energetic techniques to address various physical and energetic ailments	**Web Weaving** – Open hearts and minds who are on a journey of expanding consciousness	**Sacred Geometry** – The study of the spiritual meaning of various shapes

DNA/RNA (heal) – Spiritual energy healing modality and the most rapidly growing form of inside-out development	**Channeling** – Process of allowing an individual (the channeler) to act as a conduit or vessel for spiritual entities to communicate messages or guidance to the physical world	**"Aura" Layer Reading** – Interpreting the energy field
Astrological/Cosmos Patterning – Use the horoscope to develop the individual's awareness of the soul or enlightenment	**Past Lives (viewing)** – Able to read past lives	**True Dreaming** – Space for us to explore our deepest desires, confront our fears, and confront unresolved issues
Shaman Journey – To achieve various powers through trance or ecstatic religious experience	**Telekinetic** – Ability to move or manipulate objects with one's mind	**Apportion** – A material object that arrives suddenly and mysteriously through the powers of a medium
Pyrokinesis – Psychic ability to read, control or manipulate fire	**Retro causality (affecting physical past)** – Backwards causation is a concept of cause and effect in which an effect precedes its cause in time and so a later event affects an earlier one	**Automatic Writing** – Writing is a powerful technique you can use to channel your subconscious mind and connect with a higher source of inspiration, creativity, and insight

Out of the Body – Occurs when a person feels their consciousness depart from their physical body and enter a different realm	**Healing** – Cleansing, removal of negative thought forms, emotional pain, negativity and all negative energies	**Energy Medicine** – Permeated by an energy field that can affect our health and well-being, also called subtle energy, vibrational energy, or simply life force
Hands-on Healing – Rooted in the belief in a universal life force, facilitates wellness by manipulating the body's energy fields	**Multidimensional Healer Connections** – Existence transcends the physical realm, encompassing many dimensions and lifetimes	**Divination** – Uncover hidden knowledge by supernatural means
Intuitive (perceptive insight) – Communicate with our higher selves and connect with others on a spiritual level	**Pattering (its own)** – Accurately recognize the root system so you can connect new information, new insights, new learning, new patterns	**Recognition (past lives)** – Simple act of acknowledging a past life through a reading has the potential to alleviate karma

What are your Spiritual Gifts? (List or highlight the ones above.)

____

____

____

____

Week 4. Day 2 – Soul Blueprint (Themes)

Meditation. We can choose which meditation you want, but at least do The Liberated Healer's Zipper Energy Meditation or the Grounding Meditation.

Grab your Pendulum or use the Rosework for this exercise (40 minutes). You will review each theme, see if you get a "Yes" or a "No," and record it in this section.

Earthly Life Themes. You will only have one to four themes. We must discover our life themes now that we have gotten through the gifts. Run through this list to see what life themes you are experiencing. Through the rose exercises in this chapter or by using the pendulum, check each one and see if you get a yes or a no. This will be a big step towards learning about yourself and your life's purpose.

For example, I have two themes in this life: 1) Innovator/ Cypher, and 2) Care-er.
A cipher (or cypher) or cryptography — noun

- A secret or disguised way of writing; a code: "He/She/ Them was writing cryptic notes." A cipher is an algorithm for performing encryption or decryption — a series of well-defined steps that can be followed as a procedure. An alternative, less common term is encipherment.

What is a cipher? I admit it; when I first heard it, I had to look at what I was meant to do, which made me laugh. How could I be something I had never fully understood in English? Are you sure I wasn't meant to be a shaman, a powerful hands-on healer, or something else? Nope, and here I sit typing away, ciphering away ... into the day and the night. Thinking of all the dear souls who will get clear on their journey, I am proud of me, us, and you.

Let me explain what being a cipher means to me. The English dictionary describes it as a code or a secret way of writing. But to me, it's more than just letters on a page. It's about understanding the true intention and depth behind each word. Take "love," for example — it's a simple four-letter word, but it holds immense power and meaning when we connect it with other words or keep it close to our hearts. This is what I strive to do — to look beyond the surface and uncover the intended meanings within our language. As a cipher, my role is to interpret the messages that come through me, shedding light on complex universal concepts using the limited words we have in English. The guides often challenge me to question why we haven't created more words to capture the essence of emotions like "love fully," encouraging us to expand our vocabulary to represent such profound feelings truly.

The central theme that changed my life is learning that I am supposed to be a cipher, unlocking hidden meanings and messages beyond traditional definitions. It's an exhilarating journey as I know, comprehend, and fully embrace this gift, allowing me to dive deep into my life's purpose and calling. Each day, I eagerly anticipate whatever comes my way — the good, the bad, the happy, and the sad — so that I can fully experience and process each moment.

1. What are your Themes? Use the Rose or the Pendulum and review each item below to find the soul-specific "themes" you have come into this life with. In this section, you will find many themes. You might be surprised at what they are, but figuring this out is usually very helpful for people to understand their life's purpose. For example, I have two themes out of 54, but they are significant.

Mostly, these should all be self-explanatory in terms of their meaning. Even if the theme seems like a negative, it is not. It means you can recognize and now be that, transform it, become an expert, and own it!

irritant	manipulator	enforcer
leader	follower	loner
activator	catalyst	antagonist
aesthetic pursuits/ muse	performance	intellectuality/ researcher
persecutor	persecuted	lawfulness
victimizer	victim	justice
healer	care-er	shaman
teacher	science/rationality	analyzer
innovator/cypher	builder	pathfinder
cause fighter	humanitarian	banner carrier
experiencer	rejection	passivity
tolerance	patience	controller/handler
peacemaker	warrior/guardian	harmony
		rescuer

psychic	Spirituality	responsibility
fallibility	infallibility	fragile
survival	continuity	endurance
volunteer*	Assistant*	Traveler*

What are your Spiritual Themes? (List or highlight the ones above.) ______________________

____

____

Week 4. Day 3 – Beauty Treatment/Energy Gauges

Meditation. We can choose which meditation you want, but at least do The Liberated Healer's Zipper Energy Meditation or the Grounding Meditation.

Anti-Aging Beauty Treatments with Spirit

Everything can seem so heavy when we are working energy, so it's essential to include something fun here to lighten the mood. This goes back to the "As Above — So Below" context regarding how your physical body looks and feels, as we again are all energy!

Youth serums and treatments are all the rage these days. We see 16-year-olds getting Botox, fillers, and more, and we are not judging this, but do they know that their spiritual hygiene will make them look and feel better and much younger? Why not incorporate energy work into your vibrance plan? It's the magic ingredient. Why do significantly older adults deep into their spirituality have this youth vibrance? When they join work, they rarely get sick, and if so, it is processed out of the body so fast that they never have to stay in bed for a day.

Gina's Example: I know when I feel and look my best physically at any given time. When I was having a more challenging time and felt disconnected from Spirit, I was not living and looking the best I could. People comment on my youthful appearance daily, but they do not know that twenty years ago, I physically looked at the age I am now, which was 54 at the time of writing this. This is energy (and perhaps some natural genetics), but it does not explain why 20 years ago I looked older. I can look back at images of myself and see not only the pain in my eyes but how I carried myself and what my skin, hair, and body looked like. I might have more wrinkles on my face, but everything about me shines and vibrates. I walk in this confidence with my head held high. When I walk in a space, I command attention from anyone attracted to shine. This makes me a beacon for the light beings who want to meet me. This is true beauty. I wish more people could see that this is where they need to start, and that is with spirituality, not the very last thing they do. Congratulations again for seeing this if you've gotten this far. I have de-aged. You will de-age. It works; it is free and liberating, and you can do it as much as you want.

My Vision of myself: Long, healthy hair, a fit body where all of my joints are not in pain, and I can run and be active as needed; skin is tight and nice healthy coloring; my eyes are clear with the whites shining bright, my back and spine are elongating and not hunching over, my heart and organs are healthy, I am sleeping well with no stress energy running through me, I have a giant smile on my face, and I am surrounded by compassion and empathy for myself and the world around me.

Beauty Treatment. Draw a gold line from your heart to your higher self in Spirit. When you have guides in the further sections, you can have them do a beauty treatment for you. Imagine visions of yourself in Spirit. What does it look like? It usually will look like you in the best way you want to see yourself, whatever that is for you. Bring that version of yourself closer and closer to you to where that version of yourself is layered on top of your physical being. See the physical and the spiritual merge. Let the things holding you back from merging these versions of yourself drain out and down the grounding cord. Give yourself a bright Golden Sun and bring all this beauty and health. You can say affirmations, *"This is me and how I like to be, so may it be!"* Let any illnesses from your body fall through the grounding cord; pull them out if you must. *"If you can see it, you can be it."* It might not line up perfectly, but you always know what you are striving for; you have made the intention, and watch, people will begin to tell you, *"You look so young. Your energy is so vibrant; what has changed about you?"*

Specific Changes. You can sculpt the body and health you want here. To lose weight, highlight the area you wish to be slimmer and imagine those fat cells falling into the grounding cord and your body transforming. If you have an illness, go to that area and highlight it with light, send energy to that specific area, and watch the illness fall into the grounding cord. If you want your heart to heal, do the same: an old injury to your knees or hips, brain, and more. Do this daily. You are transforming the energy and giving specific attention to what you want to change.

List or draw what your spirit looks and feels like to manifest, aligning all parts of yourself.

____

____

Use this blank frame to draw or list what you want to manifest in your life.

Gauges – How to read percentages in your space

Gauges 0-100. Welcome to one of my favorite tools! I wished I could teach this in the first couple of days, but you needed to know the other things first. You've already learned much about energy, colors, themes, and gifts. This tool is quick to learn but mighty because we will get into the specifics in future lessons and mock-up what you want to call in.

Meditation. We can choose which meditation you want, but at least do The Liberated Healer's Zipper Energy Meditation or the Grounding Meditation.

Gauge work. When meditative, pull up a gauge with 0–100 on it, like the sample below. I like to imagine something that looks like a parking meter with a stem because we will ground this gauge to the center of the Earth. You can also give it a lovely Golden Sun to keep the energy neutral. Pull up this gauge, and let's start asking questions. The most significant thing you must practice is believing your answers and letting your intuition guide you. You will think, *"Am I just making this up?"* With practice, you will start believing what you hear, see, or know inside your energetic intelligence. This alone is building so much internal strength as you are beginning to rely on your internal guidance system. You are curating your own life at this stage. It's a great thing. Here are some starter questions, but you can start immediately on items you need clarity on.

This is the gauge that might help you, too.

Question: What is the percentage 0–100 of fear I have stuck inside my body right now?

Answer: ____

Work on changing the Percentage. If the answer was 80%, we need to get that down. While meditating, run your energy more and give yourself Golden Suns, asking to bring in more life force energy and grounding. Drop that gauge to the center of the Earth.

Pull up your rose that represents the fear in your space. Look at that rose; what color is vibrating the most? Say it's a bright red, then imagine tiny rosebuds of the same color and start to blow the little rosebuds on the larger rose. You are blowing the stuck fear energy in your space. You can even try the color flushing to get that bright red and fear out of your space. Cycle the tools; some will work better for you than others. You are harnessing what works for you; we all process differently. If you still feel very stuck, ask the guides to come in and help God/Source/Supreme Being.

Look again. Pull up another gauge that represents the fear in your space right now, and you should see a smaller percentage, even half or more. You don't have to get it down to 0 because that might not be realistic as a human. A little bit of fear is helpful because it helps us try new things and make our senses aware of dangers, but we don't want it to vibrate in our entire system. That is when we can get tired, which leads to more sickness.

Additional questions to start.

- How much male controlling energy is in my space, 0–100?
- How much female controlling energy is in my space, 0–100?
- How much other people's energy is in my space, 0–100?
- How much am I stuck in the past, 0–100?
- How much am I stuck in the future, 0–100?
- How much of my intuition am I currently open to using, 0–100?
- How much physical illness is in my body, 0–100?
- How much mental illness is my body currently processing right now, 0–100?
- How much shame am I running in my space, 0–100?

- How far along my life purpose/path, 0–100? (We will use this one soon for mock-ups/manifestations.)
- How much anger is in me, 0–100?

You can use this to ask anything; it can even be what I call a healthy addiction, as you get to see immediate change and results. There aren't many tools in life that can be this gratifying. You can go to a therapist for years and never even move the needle this much as you can when doing this work. Plus, you can do this 24/7, anytime/anywhere. You are putting your future, life, and change into your hands and control this ship now. What a wonderful thing!

Week 4. Day 4 – Mock-ups and Manifesting/ Dealing with Obstacles & Conflicts – Education

From here forward, these tools and skills are just more fun! You got through the hardest lessons of all. Now, this is the sandbox where playfulness and joy come in. Here, we are building our lives just like we want them to be. No matter your station in your life and if you want something in your heart, you have put that far away from you. Here is the time that we will systematically bring those to the forefront of your mind, body, spirit, and soul. We are going to fold these dreams back into you. It still takes time, but if you take steps daily toward the life you envisioned, you will get there.

Obstacles and Conflicts. We should all know and understand that life has a lot of obstacles and conflicts for each of us. This is a fact, and it doesn't matter what one has or doesn't have. At this point, you should address obstacles and conflicts slightly differently. It would be best if you were not impatient or rushed to judgment as fast as you used to be. What is happening is your triggers should be starting to soften. The nature of this work at moments is subtle and at moments leaps. This work, as in life, is like the ocean tide, coming in soft or coming in hard.

Energy Check-in

Ideation, Depression, and Anxiety. At this point, you should feel more connected and hopeful. It's becoming an afterthought: *"Oh, yeah, that is why I picked up this book."* The energy of confidence, seniority, and your natural birthright energy is coming back into yourself. You might be starting to daydream about a different life or existence, one where you can see what that might look like and that it is attainable. You might be dreaming while you sleep again because you are becoming liberated from the chains you or others have bound around you. Many of you had nothing to do with creating these boxes or fears that were boxing you in and making you feel stuck. You are learning that they were made of cardboard and not steel. You can break through these boxes more quickly than you initially thought. You are transmuting the hurt, pain, fear, and sadness into more positive emotions like love, joy, and happiness. Those around you should be making some comments and noticing. People are seeing that you seem different now. There is still a lot of work to be done, of course, but we are only 25 days in if you are following the program, and not many things can shift this fast in that amount of time, which is why I am a fan. I like to see progress efficiently as it makes you feel more hopeful and quicker. I am hoping that is how you are feeling right now.

Mock-ups/Manifestations

As you harness the power of energy, you can shape your reality by directing your energy towards your desires. By doing so, you signal to the universe your clear intention and open the path for support from the universe, your guides, and your higher self to manifest specific goals. We need to know precisely what you want to create; we will add a little daily at the end of your meditations. It will not be something we will do all at one time! It's a progressive, continued build to success.

Areas of Focus

Love Relationships: I would like you to take some time to envision the attributes and qualities you desire in a romantic partner. Consider how you want your partner to feel, smell, communicate, act, live, engage, care, think, work, and present themselves in various aspects of life, such as with family, friends, colleagues, and the world around them. You may also want to consider their activities, such as music, being active, enjoying comedy or poetry, and their physical characteristics. Write it down and know what you want so you can manifest it. Write what that might look like below.

____

____

____

____

Career, Life Path, School, and Work Focus: We need to break these items down and be very specific. Take a moment to consider what activity would truly excite you if you could do this for a living daily. We use the focused words "excite, excited, or excitement" and consider how different activities make you feel. For example, if you desire a promotion at work but don't enjoy your current job, getting a promotion might temporarily boost your ego but won't necessarily bring fulfillment. This exercise is about manifesting your desired life, focusing on activities that genuinely excite you.

Create a list of what a dream career would look like on a small scale.

Small scale. Create a detailed list of the items you want to obtain in the upcoming week, next week, next month, or a few months. Consider the types of projects, the people you want to work with, and the locations you want to visit for these projects. Specify the income or energy you aim to generate. Provide as many specific details as possible for each item on your list. Write what that might look like below.

Medium scale. Imagine crafting a detailed list outlining your ideal career on a medium scale. Include specific careers, jobs, or educational paths you aspire to pursue within the next six months to a year. Envision taking significant strides toward your passion. This may involve transitioning into an exciting career that ignites your enthusiasm but requires further education, financial planning, or network building. Design this roadmap to bring your vision to life. Write what that might look like below.

____

____

Large scale. Envision a career that ignites your passion and a sense of purpose every single day, driving you to eagerly rise every morning, eager to tackle your ambitious goals. This role may be a big step up that could realistically take several years or more to attain, but it's the one you are determined to achieve. It won't be without its challenges, but you will possess the skills to navigate them with grace and resilience, empowering you to create the life you've always envisioned and deserved. This career perfectly complements your true calling, offering you invaluable lessons and countless opportunities that will nurture your spirit in ways you might have never imagined. We all have the right to pursue authentic and deeply fulfilling lives. Write what that might look like below.

____

____

____

____

My Example

Small Picture: I want to share my journey of overcoming suicidal thoughts and healing Myalgic Encephalomyelitis (ME)/chronic fatigue syndrome. I aim to create content and write books to help others understand how I found healing, learned to feel comfortable in my skin, and became hopeful for the future. My goal is to inspire and offer guidance rather than pursuing a traditional 9-to-5 job with a flashy title that only provides temporary satisfaction but ultimately leads me astray.

Medium Picture: I am passionate about creating events and sharing my expertise with individuals who are eager to learn. I aim to establish connections with investors and secure funding to develop visionary programs within my envisioned ecosystem. These initiatives will have a global impact, including creating a documentary and developing a mobile and web application. I am committed to cultivating a community of individuals who are aligned with my principles, fostering a supportive and vibrant tribe. Moreover, I am dedicated to finding joy and fulfillment in collaborating with my team, colleagues, and clients.

Big Picture: I aspire to become a prominent advocate for spiritual and mental health on a global scale. I envision securing funding for numerous projects aimed at alleviating individuals' suffering. Additionally, I strive to establish a company that will provide employment opportunities for an extensive and diverse workforce. Within this organization, I am enthusiastic about fostering an environment where individuals feel valued, heard, and connected to their passions. Ultimately, I strive to generate profits while contributing to the community's betterment.

Health – Mind, Body, Emotional, Mental, and Physical: Envision the person you want to become. Identify any emotional or physical scars that need healing. Consider any aspects of your physical appearance that you would like to change. Think about cultivating a more positive inner dialogue. If you desire more energy and a youthful outlook, note that down. Reflect on handling your emotions differently, and possibly reducing or ceasing medication usage. Plan to create a more practical daily schedule and aim to improve your sleep quality. Write what that might look like below.

Family, friends, or children. If you desire to welcome children, more friends, or family into your life, you can envision them within your sphere and summon them to you. Doing this will convey your desires to the universe and help you attain them. However, due to our connections with other entities, it may be necessary to delve deeper into this process.

My example. For instance, I have long yearned to have children and build a family. This desire has been a significant challenge in my life, causing me various emotional hardships. During my spiritual journey, as I began to trust my intuition and seek guidance, I asked myself, "Why have I been unable to have children in this lifetime?" The response I received was unexpected: "Because you needed to learn how to nurture and care for yourself in this life." It suddenly clicked — my life seemed stagnant until I embraced self-love. I am taking care of my stepson and refuse to give up on my dream. I am actively working towards manifesting more stepchildren and maybe even grandchildren into my life!

Spiritual Thoughts or Experiences. Perhaps there are specific gifts or interests you're keen on nurturing. You may seek to enhance your spiritual practice, seek out a new guide, healers, or shamans to provide fresh inspiration, or recommend a transformative book that could illuminate a part of yourself you hadn't previously considered. This could help guide you toward spiritual healing or provide additional necessary tools. You are discovering like-minded individuals interested in collaborating within this realm and establishing a supportive community to explore these exciting and safe ventures. Write what that might look like below.

____

____

____

____

Week 4. Day 5 – Mock-ups and Manifesting Exercise

Exercise: Mock-ups and Manifestations

Meditation. We can choose which meditation you want, but at least do The Liberated Healer's Zipper Energy Meditation or the Grounding Meditation. ***This is a 30 to 45-minute practice.***

- **Visualize.** To begin, visualize a giant soap bubble just outside your aura.
- **Focus.** Within this bubble, focus on the specific thing you want to create or manifest. Avoid overcrowding the bubble with too many details, which may hinder the manifestation process.

- **Grounding.** Next, add a grounding cord to release any energy impeding your manifestation and send it to the center of the Earth.
- **Be specific about the details**, including when, where, and the desired outcome, and seal it with your signature and even a date on which you want that thing to manifest.
    - Putting their name or picture inside the bubble is okay if it's a specific person or energy.
    - If it's a specific contract or amount, or even if you want the money to go into your bank, you can envision your bank account full of an amount.
- **Drain the Energy.** Once done, release any drained energy and replenish it with a few Golden Suns, giving it life. You can add emotions, such as love, joy, happiness, or colors that represent that for you.
- **Protection.** Lastly, encase the bubble with a protective rose on the outside of it.
- **Copy.** Create multiple copies of the bubble as we spread these throughout the universe.
- **Blessing.** Say a blessing, *"May it be with the blessing of God/Source/Supreme Being that this gets to who or where it needs to go to help my growth, and so the universe knows this is what I want to manifest."*
- **For love.** Say you want someone who might not be able to come into your life for one reason or another, but you want someone like that; we would then say, *"Please manifest this person ______________ or someone on that level or even a level up in their vibration."*
- **For career.** You can even add the salary or contract you want to attract.
- **Cut the cord.** Use giant scissors to cut the grounding cord and release the bubbles across the universe, letting them fly off and away.

- **Gauge.** After completing these steps, assess your feelings using your gauge about the specific thing you asked for, ranging from 0 to 100. If you are likely to receive this thing, you can add a Golden Sun over the gauge and a grounding cord, or you can go and do the **"Rosework"** for a deeper look at what mind is hindering you from moving forward. They all work together, and there isn't any way you can do this wrong.
- **Repeat** if the desired manifestation is not reflected in your emotions.
- **Intention.** Finally, affirm your intention for the desired vibration while releasing energy for things you do not want.

Mock-up for Others: You can also do this for others, but everyone has **FREE WILL**, so leave space for them to change it or not have it. For example, if someone is sick and you want to see them get well, you can do rosework on them "With their Permission" or create a Mock-up where you see them healed.

How to Find Something that Has Been Lost or Stolen. You can create a bubble for the missing or stolen project, request it be returned to you, and sign the bubble. Try to release down the grounding cord the tension or pain about the thing you lost or the shame that you trusted someone who has this taken from you. **This can be very triggering for you, and if you are not ready to do this, it's okay, as betrayal is very hard to process.**

TIP: Sometimes, there are blocks from receiving what you want in your life in unhealed wounds; a mental block tells you you cannot have that. That is the energy that might be in your space. This is very common. It's okay; that is why we are here doing the work. Go back to the rosework and see what the blockages are. Here are some examples.

- You don't believe that you can have what you want. Resistance is the #1 reason people stop their healing journey.
- You are afraid if you get the thing you want, you might lose it, so it's better not to have it at all. This can be related to an abandonment or a neglected wound.
- You are at a different frequency than the thing or person you want. For example, you might want someone vibrating even higher or lower than you are now. You can look at your energy and theirs with the gauge to see where each of you is. If they are at a lower frequency, you can only pray and send positive support for their spiritual journey. If they are at a higher frequency than you, you know what you need to do ... more energy work.
- Ask your higher self to be neutral about the outcome so you do not create resistance in your space for what you want.
- Keep asking away, uncover what the blockages are, and release them.

Keep up the excellent work in creating the life you desire. It's important to remember that this process requires practice. You may discover new approaches or additional methods that resonate with you. These are guidelines, not rigid rules, so feel free to experiment and enjoy the journey. Above all, approach this with enthusiasm and excitement!

Week 4. Day 6 – Calm Meditations

Meditation is a word that is known to most people now. Why is it all the talk? Because it's what a human needs, especially in this modern age of technology. It aligns the mind, body, soul, and spirit so they collapse into each other. When we are one, we can make changes more rapidly and see the roads ahead much better and which paths are speaking to our hearts; we go in and see the wounds and put loving care and attention around them so they can heal.

Do you ever recall a day you binge-watched television or social media and said to yourself, "Wow, that was a great memory and experience; I want to remember that day forever"?

For the World's Children, We Must Change Ourselves as Adults

Comparison energy. The concept of "comparison energy" highlights the tendency for individuals, particularly children, to emulate the behaviors and attitudes of adults. This phenomenon has a profound impact, and we must combat it to protect the world's children. If you find it challenging to address this issue for yourself, consider using the well-being of children as a motivating force. The struggle against comparison energy is not new; it has been an enduring part of human experience, driving us to strive for the lives and experiences we desire as individuals. However, the rise of social media has transformed this energy into something entirely different. We must actively work to resist the urge to compare ourselves to others. This is also an area I needed help with.

This phenomenon contributes to the distress and harm experienced by our children. As responsible adults, safeguarding the well-being of children must be our utmost priority. It is essential to educate others about comparison energy and teach them effective strategies for redirecting their thoughts when such feelings arise. These are crucial tools for navigating today's world and the future.

As we transition from the "Material Age" to the "Age of Aquarius," there is a growing emphasis on what truly holds value. I envision a future where individuals grow weary of consuming content that offers no natural enrichment. Instead, they will seek solace in nature. It's important to note that some individuals exist to divert our attention, often without awareness of their impact on society. These individuals remain fixated on superficial aspects of identity and are elevated to a societal pedestal. While they have their paths to follow, their influence on millions perpetuates a message of "you lack what I possess," undermining the inherent worth of every individual. Redirecting this collective energy and focus toward addressing global issues could lead us to a utopian society.

Remember, your energy allocation reflects your spending habits. By promoting, consuming, and purchasing the products associated with specific individuals, you essentially fuel their wealth and prosperity. They have mastered the art of diverting attention from oneself and capitalizing on others' resources and happiness.

Rose/Gauge Work on Comparison/Competitive Energy

Please use your tools today to measure how much "comparison energy" you hold inside yourself, ranging from 0 to 100. Pull this out; it will feel so good! Again, it is natural to have some of this energy to motivate us, but not at our current levels. Thanks, social media!

Imagine a rose in front of you and ground it to the center of the Earth. Ask your spirit to pull out all your comparison energy and throw it into that rose. Drop it into the lava. Please do it again until you reach a reasonable level of comparison energy in your space. Please give yourself a Golden Sun, recalling all your energy from everyone else you gave it to to create and manifest more of the life you want.

"Where your attention goes is who is getting richer and raising their bank account while yours is dwindling. Call it back to you!"

My Daily Process

To support your healing journey, I'd like to share my own experience with you. Maybe my story can spark some ideas for you or help you recognize some of the positive techniques you may already use. There was a time in my life when I experienced PTSD every morning. I had to find ways to calm my body and mind to get out of bed. Despite the temptation to rely on medication, I made a conscious decision not to go down that path. It was challenging at first, but I'm thankful that I was able to manage without medication. If the situation had persisted much longer, I might have reconsidered, but thankfully, the practices I adopted improved my mornings. Eventually, the frequency of my panic attacks decreased significantly, and I rarely woke up to them anymore.

Morning Practice. First, hug yourself and others around you if that is your situation. Stretch your arms and legs, look at your hands and feet (if you can), and notice they are alive. Imagine what they might do or create on this day ahead of you. Look around the room and see your space and any other living beings and offer them energetic love, including your partner, children, family members, animals, and even your living plants. Say with deep conviction and power, "Hello, I love you." The word "Hello" holds great power in its spiritual intention. We will address this in later meditations.

- Play meditation music on low so it's not overpowering but lays a calming vibration throughout your space.
- Invite the phrase (either out loud or internally): "I am so grateful and excited that I get to…" and list the people, projects, and things you will be interacting with that day. This will create a high-energy vibration throughout the day and for everyone you mention.

Midday Practice. When you experience tension, anxiety, or fear, remind yourself that you have everything you need to remain centered in your energy. Invite the phrase (either out loud or internally): "I am anxious about this ____________ ____________________________, but I have all the tools to succeed. No matter what happens, it will be a valuable experience in my life." Even if doubt arises, you can speak these words to increase a positive vibration.

Evening Practice. Take three deep breaths in and out; reflect on what happened that day and speak, imagine, or journal about these events. Checking in with yourself increases self-awareness and enhances the ability to pay attention to daily lessons. Honor yourself for being present and trying to move through your life. Finding things that work for you as an individual to close out the day is essential. You might want to do a crossword, read, or take a short walk. Whatever it is, try to find at least one customary thing you like to do. The schedule helps to ground us, especially when we are in moments of depression or other negative states.

Ho'oponopono (sounds like HO.O.PO.NO.PO.NO) Forgiveness Practice

(5–10 minutes)

This is one of my favorite practices. I do it often in my own life and encourage my clients to do the same. It is a traditional Hawaiian practice centered around reconciliation, forgiveness, and mental cleansing. It is used to put things back correctly through adjustments, amending, and rectifying "to make good." Because conflict occurs from different people's perspectives, using intentional empathy to imagine being the other person and understanding how they may have perceived the conflict can expand the practice and enhance its benefits.

Practice. There are a few variations online, including a larger version that the Hawaiians use, but here is the standard practice.

Sit comfortably, close your eyes, and let your breath find your natural rhythm. With each exhale, allow any tension to drain from the body.

Address what you want to heal, practice, or forgive any transgressions you wish to release, including persons or groups involved — no matter who is believed to be at fault. You can say in your mind or aloud whichever of the following statements feels most potent. As you say one or several, feel the emotion behind the words.

"I'm sorry." "Please forgive me." "Thank you." "I love you." "I wish you peace."

Repeat these statements over and over for as long as you can, up to 108 repetitions, which in Tibetan Buddhism is a number that connects us to ourselves and the world and universe around us.

At the end of the practice, take a moment to journal your reflections on what you felt before and after the training in your body and mind:

Week 4. Day 7 – Integration Day – Growth Periods/ Working Through the Resistance Education

Meditation. We can choose which meditation you want, but at least do The Liberated Healer's Zipper Energy Meditation, Grounding Meditation, or the other calming meditations given as options for you (20 minutes minimum before this work).

When you're moving into "effort." I'm reflecting on something that bothered me and needs to be addressed here. I consider myself a highly productive person, and when I'm determined to accomplish something, I tackle it with great intensity. I expected to see immediate results from my efforts, but there were days when I felt incredibly uplifted and others when I felt unfortunate. I've realized that experiencing these highs and lows is an inevitable part of the journey, and I'm pushing myself as hard as possible. I've understood that this is a long-term commitment, not a sprint. Despite the challenges, I know that I will eventually reach my goals and continue to learn and apply the tools I have acquired. Over time, these tools will become integral to who I am and my spiritual arsenal. That is when I learned I was going into "effort." Oh darn, that crazy effort — trying to make something happen before it's time!

Everything Has Its Timing – You Must Be Patient – Temperance is Necessary!

As detailed in the previous days, we are working with the guidance of a spiritual team that has supported us throughout lifetimes and many collaborations. They often visit us in dreamtime and subtly guide us during meditation.

In my first book, *Surviving Suicidal Ideation: From Therapy to Spirituality and the Lived Experience,* I openly discussed the physical and mental abuse I endured in my childhood. These experiences shaped my adult life, and I found myself carrying the themes of unworthiness and fear of abandonment like badges I proudly wore around my head and heart. It wasn't until I started my healing journey that I realized I was attracting similar energy and situations into my life. Until I learned the lessons from these experiences, set new boundaries, and welcomed new people, projects, and energies into my life, I was stuck in a pattern of repeating negative experiences.

Looking back, I find it amusing and bewildering why humans, including myself, can be stubborn when learning and growing. I discovered that we are inherently programmed to survive through discussions with highly trained individuals and therapists. Although we may not be fighting for survival physically like our ancestors, we still compete for jobs, mates, and resources. However, unlike in the past, we now have access to advanced thinking and tools that allow us to recognize destructive patterns and make healthier choices. This guidebook is rooted in profound love, compassion, and empathy for anyone who reads it. It is intended to offer a warm bath of love, kindness, and etheric support for the reader. I encourage you to let the words and images wash over you and embrace the healing from tears. Each tear symbolizes release and reminds you of what makes you uniquely human.

Growth Periods

As we journey through life, we experience periods of spiritual growth like the physical "growing pains" we faced as children. It's comforting to know that we are not alone in this process and that there are healers, shamans, and supportive individuals we can turn to during these times of growth. While it may feel daunting, embracing these experiences and recognizing that they are part of our personal and unique spiritual journey is important.

Embracing our humanity and allowing ourselves to navigate our spiritual development with kindness and self-compassion is crucial. As we deepen our connection with the divine and navigate the various stages of growth, it's essential to move with the rhythm of the energy, allowing ourselves to express our emotions and acknowledge our inner strength. This ongoing evolution is not fixed but rather a dynamic process that requires patience and self-appreciation.

Each step we take on this path is a testament to our resilience, and we should take pride in our efforts and marvel at our inner strength.

Stages of Spiritual Growth

Usually, you would have been given these stages of spiritual growth earlier, but we did this later so you can see how far you have come. We are now leaning into stages 6 and 7 in the next month. Congratulations on getting through the first month. You have accomplished so much.

1. A complete absence of awareness and connection to your spiritual self.
2. A recognition or remembrance that there is more than the material world.
3. Spiritual curiosity — a thirst to learn more about the spirit and our spiritual self.
4. Spiritual exploration and study.
5. Developing a spiritual practice.
6. An acceptance of yourself and others.
7. Spiritual maturity and Dark Night of the Soul.

If your growth periods have been too intense, let the universe and your spirit know you want a different way to receive your lessons.

Dear Universe or Spirit,

"I am choosing to experience life lessons more in JOY than PAIN. I want my spiritual growth to stay within a gradual expansion. May the lessons be tempered gently."

Congratulations on reaching this milestone! The first thirty days may have been challenging, but you did it. It's essential to be gentle with yourself during this time. Nourish your body with nutrient-rich foods like fruits, vegetables, and plants. When you need to recharge, consider taking brisk walks to invigorate your energy or indulging in a relaxing bath to immerse yourself in the soothing embrace of water. I hope this period of your life is filled with blessings and all your aspirations come to fruition. May you deepen your love for yourself and embrace your unique qualities and energy, recognizing the significance of your presence on this planet. Your existence is truly magical, and I want nothing but your most fulfilling experiences. Consider these words a warm embrace and a high-five to celebrate your remarkable achievement!

SEA HORSE – Week 5 – We Are the Creators of Our Experience, Soul Contracts, Twin Flames, Soulmates, Ego, Identity, Death and Rebirth

This week, the Sea Horse is our Spirit Animal, holding space for us as we traverse the seas of change.

I call in the essence of tranquil divine love that is safe and trusted,
like the elegant seahorse that traverses the sea like a magical unicorn.
I love you; you love me; we love each other in trinity.
Let's search for the beauty in the world.

Week 5. Day 1 – Soul Contracts/Agreements, Identity, Ego Blindness, Suicide, and Twin Flames

The Earth is a wondrous place for cycling. Our planet is teeming with many animal and plant species and a rich tapestry of human cultures. Despite facing challenging circumstances, being present here is a precious blessing. At the heart of it all, love connects us.

– *Gina Cavalier*

We are the Creator of our life experience; Souls are Born, and others are cycling.

Meditation. We can choose which meditation you want, but at least do The Liberated Healer's Zipper Energy Meditation, Grounding Meditation, or the other calming meditations given as options for you (20 minutes minimum before this work).

The journey of the soul is a fascinating one. Souls are constantly growing and evolving through their experiences in different lifetimes. As they go through each incarnation, their persona, memories, and impressions are shaped and stored within their consciousness. It's like waking up from a dream and having a vague impression of the characters and events. The soul retains the essence of these experiences but lets go of the specific details of each lifetime's identity. This continuous process of growth and evolution allows the soul to ascend the ladder of consciousness, becoming more refined and evolved with each incarnation.

As the soul progresses, it gains power, energy, and intelligence, ultimately transforming into a greater being known as an Oversoul. As discussed earlier, we will dive in further here. The Oversoul can simultaneously experience multiple lifetimes, allowing it to learn and expand from various perspectives at an accelerated rate. Every soul is on this evolutionary journey; some move through it more quickly due to their intentional choices, while others progress slowly. The soul's journey is a remarkable and ongoing process of growth and enlightenment.

Identity Being Wiped

Throughout our diverse lifetimes, we have all entertained the idea of indulging in mischief. No one can claim complete innocence; in some way, we are all complicit, all on a journey of exploration together. It's as if we are watching a movie designed to elevate our awareness and steer us toward rediscovering our authentic selves in fresh and exhilarating ways, igniting our creativity and innovation. This drives the universe's expansion — the myriad perspectives, experiences, and possibilities that emerge from us and other sentient beings. As we evolve, we will eventually transcend the need to learn from these negative themes. We must allow these energies to run their course and respond positively and skillfully. In time, the negative energy will diminish, and its extreme manifestations on Earth will fade. We will live in a more Utopian society where all souls are cared for in a balanced expression, with massive creativity, new species being born, and communications with other outward energies sharing technology and advice. We were ultimately built for it and can make small strides to get everyone there. Do not diminish your role here and how importantly your one soul and expression can enhance the planet.

You and Your Soul Family Mapped Your Adventure

It is an honor to come to Earth and work here; it is known to be one of the most complex but most rewarding places to grow one's soul's intelligence. We have a core group of souls that we will cycle through in this life. Some are in other phases and might not be here physically, but they are always a part of helping guide us from the most loving place. When you learn to recognize energy deeper, you will know who these people are when you meet them. There will be many signs that speak to you individually. You might dream about them before, during, or immediately after meeting them. Your heart might race when you meet them or get tingly all over. Your body is trying to use your senses to give you signals to go towards that person; that is where your next lesson is. It can be a scary and exciting thing. Nobody likes being uncomfortable, but it is where we grow the most. Let me say that I am sorry for the hardships we all must go through. I have recently started to ask spirit: You are giving it the direction that I have reached my maximum pain threshold for life lessons. To bring in more straightforward lessons. As souls, we can be overzealous and bold, saying, "I can handle anything; bring it all on." Then, realize that it is not easy. Let's call in some kinder, more effortless, gentler lessons, shall we?

In our lives, the individuals within our soul family often take on different roles, saying to each other, "This time, I'll be the brother, sister, mother, aunt, boyfriend, girlfriend, wife, husband."

Many spiritualists and those who have had near-death experiences elaborate on this concept with fierce agreement. It may be hard to fathom, but they suggest that we actively planned many of the most challenging experiences we have endured. Conversely, we also planned the joyful aspects of our lives, such as marriages, children, careers, travels, encounters with animals, experiences in the natural world, accomplishments, and the kindness of strangers. This cosmic dance between darkness and light is always present.

Specific moments in our lives are carefully plotted like benchmarks, but due to our free will, we may take a long or short time to reach each one, and some may need to be explained. It's crucial to remain attentive to the shifts in our lives and remember when and who is involved. We will try to list these souls below.

We Get Stuck

We know in our souls when it is time to move out of a relationship to get new experiences, but it can be terrifying. There is no judgment if one decides to stay in a lifelong commitment to someone else even if they were only intended to be with that person momentarily because those lessons will come in another form, in another way, at another time. Still, inside, you will know using your intuition that you were meant to go down a road that was not expressed. But at least know this is better than just being blind to it all. Your soul will still try to find ways to say things and turn that way a bit; there is something you can see, hear, or feel. There is no wrong or right way; there is only ... your way.

Ego Blindness

If you are here, you want to evolve and change your circumstances in life. Use the time you are here to become the best human being on this planet and understand why your soul has journeyed here. At this point, a part of your ego and identity will die, and you cherish that part. That part was a colleague, a friend, a guide, and it had its purpose, but it also brought you habits that might have made you codependent, disconnected, rageful, angry, and lost. This program brings you home to yourself first, then your spiritual family (as above), and then back again here in the physical (as below). You will be different at the end of this program; you will be tuned to the vibration of the Planet.

I giggle and shake my head as I wonder why humans are so stubborn in learning and growing, and I was one of them. Through many of my discussions with highly trained individuals, PhDs, and therapists, the simple answer is that we are programmed to survive. Maybe we are not surviving in a cold cave anymore, but we are fighting for the same jobs, mates, and resources and are instinctually driven to be the last one on top of that hill. The difference now is that we have access to advanced thinking and tools that take us out of the Renaissance times, and we can recognize these destructive patterns in ourselves and others. We can choose to calm our egos for healthier choices that help us first and the world around us. We can find peaceful resolutions through harsh conflicts and conversations because we can see beyond ourselves and how our energy affects everything. Let the words and images wash over you like a warm bath of love, kindness, and etheric support. Feel the healing through your tears if needed. See each tear as a gift of release and what makes you uniquely you and human.

This guidebook is created from the most profound love, compassion, and empathy levels for you.

I mentioned this in the introduction, but it bears repeating. Since this book is more of a short-list of the themes for an overall handbook for the living, we are not taking deep dives into each category. The resource section in the back will have recommended books from experts, authors, and teachers investigating, exploring, and explaining the more prominent themes mentioned.

Suicide Questions/Contracts

The concept of suicide as a pre-incarnation choice for certain souls is tricky to grasp. It presents the idea that life is like a movie, with each person playing a role so convincingly that they forget they are actors. Some souls may choose a path of suicide as part of their predestined story, not out of negativity or spite, but as a learning experience for themselves and others around them. It emphasizes the importance of supporting individuals to keep them healthy and safe while acknowledging that certain aspects of life are beyond our control. Ultimately, it encourages a sense of interconnectedness and understanding within the greater flow of life. I have seen, though, a lot of souls who checked out early because they were too sensitive to the density of Planet Earth. They watch what the world is doing to animals, lose skills in ritual, community, family, abuses, and betrayals, and it grows to social contagion. It can be challenging to stay here when you are a sensitive soul. That is why we must be kinder, avoid divisive conversations, and stop focusing too much on things that separate us as a humanity, like politics and more.

Question: What happens when one commits suicide? Do we incarnate again to come back to finish our contract?

Answer: There is always a choice between incarnations. To assume otherwise would imply that you are powerless. God can't be anything other than love. There is always a choice.

Please ask yourselves if you would like to come back. There are no forced incarnations; you choose it because you love the expansion and the learning. Sometimes, you decide to return immediately; it is always your choice. It is your body; you determine what you do with it. Suicide can be a dramatic way out of the story that you have created, yes. There are many other ways to achieve the same goal — it is not correct or wrong — it is simply an act. This often occurs when a soul is tired and discouraged; you feel lost, connected, and disconnected, and your forgetting is so deep, so well into the darkness, you can't go on. There is nothing to forgive, dear ones and nothing to release. You create your bodies, and you do with them what you will.

Suicidal Ideation Can Be an Energetic War

The journey of souls is complex, filled with contracts and free will. Some souls fulfill their contracts, others engage in an energetic struggle, and some depart prematurely, choosing to cycle out more quickly than planned. We contract with other souls to achieve specific life goals, but sometimes, they decide not to honor these agreements, leaving our hearts and souls feeling broken. For example, imagine having a soul contract to meet your twin flame and have a child together, but your twin flame is trapped in a toxic karmic relationship that prevents them from being with you. This situation can seem disheartening, but we are encouraged to practice soul-soothing tools and believe that better things are on the horizon. Despite the challenges, we are supported by the spirit, and if we persevere, a more aligned soul will come into our lives. This requires patience, which can be especially difficult for humans who have become increasingly disconnected from nature and immersed in the energy of urban environments.

Addiction Energy (Low Vibrational Energies)

They (my guides) are repeating this from the introduction. Please know this: Just because suicide can feel like an energy of darkness, it doesn't mean anyone who does this will end up in the darkness. Their soul will always go back home to love. They want to help us stop this pattern and explain why some energies are here supporting me and helping others.

Addressing this aspect of energy is essential, although it may be challenging to discuss. I will briefly mention it to avoid triggering too many people and will delve into it further in future work. It's essential to remember that energy healing can quickly change and improve this aspect. When a person is vibrating with addiction, their aura can attract lower entities that are not beneficial for spiritual well-being. It is crucial to address and heal these addictions in any way possible and focus on improving one's energy so that these negative influences can no longer hold on. My heart goes out to those struggling with any form of addiction. We must extend our love and compassion to them and ask for healing light to surround them instead of passing judgment. They are suffering and in need of support and love.

These entities exploit human desires that the soul seeks to understand, creating a tangled web in the aura through which darker, lower entities can infiltrate. They make a slow form of self-destruction on this plane. Although the person may not necessarily intend to end their life, they are slowly harming themselves knowingly. It's as if they become a plaything for these entities, controlled and influenced by darkness, which gradually engulfs them until their body gives in. This form of self-destruction is only sometimes recognized as such, reflecting the patterns we have adopted in this life. This aspect is often overlooked when considering suicide, as these entities may take over individuals. However, engaging in spiritual work can remove these entities; they cannot remain with those dedicated to this practice!

Sometimes, the soul realizes that if they leave this world in the physical, they will be taking these entities with them and sometimes eliminating generations of curses and eliminating them from others' ancestors with them — almost like being a stealth fighter that drags the enemy out. There needs to be a re-education on suicide to trust and honor our souls. We need to work with the energy of the light and God to transmute these things. The guides want this not just for those people who are suffering but for those who are left behind, as they can be incredibly tortured. This happens because of this doctrine dogma propaganda that is believed and pushed around to those who are gone.

If you are here reading this right now, it is not a fluke; my guides have put you on this path to heal yourself and others collectively. They want to share all these understandings with you.

Suicidal Past Lives, Healing It in This Life

A good amount of people who have suicidal ideation in this life had previously been suicidal or died in this way in a past life, and this is a theme that needs to be healed. It is almost like an ECHO from the past. That energy is resolved through your skillful response to it in this life, not engaging with it from a victim mentality but through a healthy perspective of healing and creativity. There are also studies that they are doing now that show it could also be in your genes, so it is good that they are starting to take this topic seriously and putting funding toward learning more about it.

Twin Flames in the Heat of Passion and the deepest love between two people.

Twin Flames

Twin flames are undeniably real. They are like two sides of the same coin, sharing remarkable similarities. When they come together, an overwhelming rush of intense emotions is inevitable. Their connection transcends time, and they can communicate with each other telepathically. Often, they can sit in silence for hours and still engage in deep, meaningful conversations.

However, encountering a twin flame in this lifetime does not guarantee a romantic relationship. The intense energy and the soul's pre-existing programming can create fear and hesitation, potentially preventing the relationship from blossoming. I met one of my twin flames who is in a marriage that has lived past it's time, but due to religious reasons (which I respected), this person was too afraid to leave even though they were miserable and in a surface-level union. There is no judgment again, just an explanation. I totally understood, moving away from those things when you have been heavily pressured is complex and a part of their journey. Just appreciate the love and let it go into the light. Often, this energy will come in and we will have full conversations, and I am just happy that I got to meet them in person. We had the same hands and the same eyes. It was an undeniable connection.

One of my Twin Flames' matching thumbs.

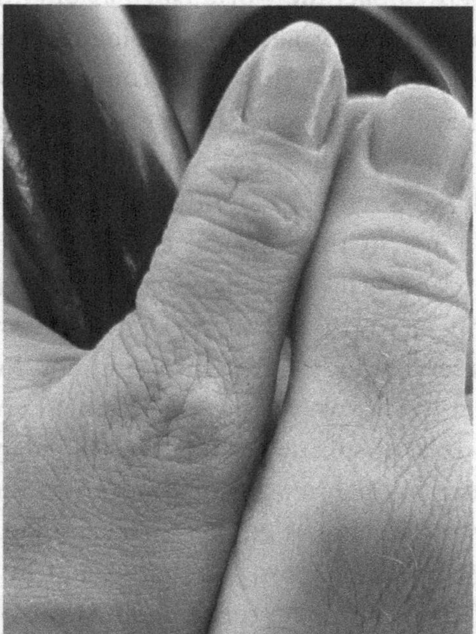

It is possible to have multiple twin flames, though not an endless number. Depending on our paths, we may encounter two, three, four, or even five such connections in our lifetime. Our choices and free will play a significant role in determining whether we will meet these individuals. If you do get to share physical, intimate relations with your twin flame, you will never be the same. Your spiritual activation will get heightened in ways you had no idea it was possible. There are no drugs here, but you will be flying high, and you will want to capture that feeling and bottle it if you can.

- Yes, twin flames are different from karmic and soulmates, which will be detailed in the next section.
- Twin flames are souls with whom we share deep connections across multiple lifetimes. While these connections are often romantic, they can also manifest as sibling relationships, partnerships, and colleagues to positively impact the world, such as building a business or creating transformative technologies to help the earth.
- The reasons behind these soul connections are twofold. First, they involve cycling through experiences with these beloved souls, and second, they are about not wanting to undergo a wholly individuated existence. Even if we haven't met in the physical realm, our souls continue to learn and grow together. Yes, you meet often in the heavenly or spiritual realm to share and connect.
- Encounters with twin flames are not limited to the physical world; we often connect and share experiences in the astral or spiritual realm. This can manifest through vivid dreams before, during, and after our interactions with them, serving as guided messages and a pathway to deeper connections. Yes, you share a soul, but it's not 100% shared. This makes no sense, then. How can your soul's

records, information, and knowledge be continued? It's just about 10% of an overlap of a shared soul so you can find each other and learn from each other's lives again.

- The intense love and emotions associated with twin flames can be overwhelming, leading to sleepless nights and obsessive thoughts. This is our soul's way of remembering and craving the profound love often challenging in our physical reality.
- The dynamic of a "runner" and a "chaser" in twin flame relationships is familiar. It arises from both individuals being at different spiritual stages, with one being more spiritually advanced than the other. The "chaser" is usually the one who is more prepared for union, while the "runner" may need more time to catch up. It's a lesson in patience, growth, and understanding divine timing.
- The intensity of the connection can trigger biological and brain chemistry responses, contributing to the overwhelming feelings experienced in these relationships. Despite the challenges, these connections offer profound opportunities for growth and learning.
- I've met my twin flame at pivotal moments when I've been at a crossroads, and it feels like the universe is guiding us in a new positive direction. For instance, one of my twin flames and I instantly recognized each other's energy at an event. He was amid a 13-year marriage separation but hadn't decided to move out. He was unhappy for a long time, and he had even mentioned this to a friend from whom I met this person. Although he seriously considered leaving for good when we met, he ultimately chose to stay, which I respected. I am happy about this connection, and I have never had a physical display of our affections. Even though we didn't end up together, I still send him love, knowing we share a deep soul connection.

He firmly believed in our twin flame bond; we both had dreams and memories of separated souls.

- Another twin flame I recently met is also going through a separation but not yet divorced. One person is always at a severe crossroads; the other has already crossed that experience off their list and learned from it. He has been hesitant about embracing the twin flame concept, but our meeting has sparked a profound spiritual awakening for both of us. We even shared detailed dreams of each other on the night we met, which felt surreal. I feel fortunate to understand the dynamics of twin flame connections, as it has helped me navigate these intense experiences. The connection is extraordinary and requires immense patience and spiritual work. I've come to understand that each person has free will, so the best I can do is send them off with loving thoughts, perhaps an occasional grounding cord, and prayer.
- Do twin flames share similar physical attributes? Most often, yes. You will share a birthmark, eyes, colors, shapes, and, oddly enough, hands and fingers, especially thumbs. Put them together and see what it looks like!
- You would like to have many past lives. Try reading about your and this person's past lives. They might blow you away and make you more spiritually awake.

In cases where the connection is also a soulmate bond with karmic ties, I believe in the potential for relationship healing by transmuting karma. I'm preparing to attend a class on this soon, and I know that roses will be involved in that transformative work.

Some of the feelings of the Twin Flame Experience:

- **Yearning and Longing.** Something is speaking to you where you begin to long for a deep love, and you want to find it. You may be having intense dreams of love, even sexual encounters in your sleep. Your twin flame is on the horizon, and they are making changes in their life right now, maybe to meet you.
- **The meeting.** The universe has a trick up its sleeve, aligning you to meet. Looking back, you will be mesmerized by how it all aligned. When you entered the space, you were directed to them, how your eyes met, every little detail. There will be signs and dreams, and it will feel momentarily as if time has stopped because it has momentarily. You made a massive shift into a new experience and an upgrade in spirituality.
- **Awakening and connection.** This time will vary significantly due to all the different circumstances. Suppose you are lucky enough to be able to connect physically, either by holding hands, kissing, more, or even just meditating together. In that case, you will both be put on a different road.
- **Challenges and triggers.** Grab your seatbelts. It will also be emotional; knowing these stages is essential, especially if you have old relationship wounds. This one will trigger all those, and you must move through it as gracefully as possible. You both won't be in the same place, and might flip and flop around. There will be a common knowing through it all, though, that you love one another deeply; you probably won't say it, but not for a long time. This one is different.

Stages:

- **Someone is the Runner, and someone is the Chaser.** Then, it can switch back and forth for a while (it feels like an eternity, and sometimes it is).
- **Remove walls and go into vulnerability.** You both suddenly feel safe and trusted in each other's energy.
- **Surrender and healing. If you get to this place with your twin flame, you have won the soul lottery.** It takes work, and not many can get through all the pain it takes to make this intense relationship work. It's because you are a mirror for each other, which can repel you momentarily until you heal.

Have you ever met anyone that this seems like a fit? Please list out their attributes and how the meeting happened. If you dream of someone who could be this, list them with as much detail as possible.

Please use your rose and gauge to ask questions and get answers.

We Go Together – Twin separation feels like a death.

When Twins Part

When twins part or cannot be together, this is what it looks like in Spirit. There is an intense longing. Often, you will meet a twin when you are married or just coming out of a divorce. It is for you to make a free will choice to expand your spirituality, but they will often run because the energy is too intense. Sometimes they come back, but often not, which is why it is the most beautiful expression of romantic love but also the hardest. I have had this happen to me twice, once in 2023, and once this year in 2024. This is why I confirmed the "knowing" that there can be more than one twin, which makes sense.

Week 5. Day 2 – Soulmates, Karmic Relationships (Karma and Dharma), and Practice

Meditation. We can choose which meditation you want, but at least do The Liberated Healer's Zipper Energy Meditation, Grounding Meditation, or the other calming meditations given as options for you (20 minutes minimum before this work).

We mentioned this briefly in yesterday's work, but it needs to be repeated. This passage delves into pre-incarnation, where souls come together to plan and coordinate their intentions during their shared incarnational experiences. It explores the idea that individuals, other souls, and family members organize specific details of their interactions, often exchanging roles to gain insight from different perspectives. The text also discusses how the universe provides signs and nudges to guide individuals back to their intended paths if they veer off course.

The Laws of Karma versus Dharma Soulmate Contract

You are not kind in all your lives. We have been good and bad as we strengthen and witness ourselves from positions of power and non-power lives. The physical body is the only way to work on your karma. Once you return to the spiritual realm, you can gain knowledge but cannot influence anything or anyone or correct your past actions. That's why this life and body are highly significant. Even when faced with challenges, it's crucial to confront them directly. You have the support to overcome them.

The goal is to get more into the state of dharma, which means gaining life lessons and fulfilling relationships to the point where there isn't a karmic lesson. The "Wheel of Karma" is accurate, but we need both sides to recognize what is right, or we will not know the difference. Do not resist this knowledge. We should be respecting the soul work we are all here to do. You will see everything you did and said and how you affected each person when you pass your life review (teaching in a later section). Don't you want to work on this now in the present, but get to a better place in this life while you have the opportunity?

Have you ever met anyone who you instantly didn't like? They just rubbed you the wrong way. Instead of running from those people, you should probably dig in and find out why you had that reaction. Most likely, there was a past life and some karma attached to the both of you. If you can subtly unpack this and turn it around, you have won the game of karma. You can heal from the past life and create a better future now. If we knew this more, we could work through so much more than we are today.

Understanding karmic lesson relationships can be challenging. These are connections with individuals we have soulmate contracts with, meaning we are destined to do significant work together, such as building families, businesses, and more. These relationships are intertwined with karmic lessons of reciprocity, and the souls involved have likely interacted before. It's important to note that these connections are distinct from twin flame relationships. Each soul's journey cycles in and out of our soul family circle. These relationships teach us important lessons, and although they may feel intense and captivating, they are ultimately meant to facilitate our growth. Identifying the lessons we are meant to learn together is crucial, as it helps us avoid creating new karma. These connections manifest as lifelong relationships with family members or friends, often rooted in conflict or competition. Recognizing this dynamic and working to heal from it is essential for our personal growth. These karmic lesson relationships are among the most significant on our journey, second only to twin flame connections. While there is no limit to the number of soulmates we can encounter, individuals with assertive spirits may question why they chose to engage with so many soulmates in this lifetime.

Karmic soulmates are deeply connected individuals whose relationship is intense, transformative, and often accompanied by significant emotional pain. They profoundly impact each other's lives and frequently catalyze spiritual growth and self-discovery. These relationships typically arise to resolve unresolved issues or trauma from past lives with that soul energy. For example, you may relate to prevalent power struggles and competition. This could reflect a past life where you and your partner were engaged in similar dynamics. In this life, you can clear that karmic residue and learn to love unconditionally despite any past hurt or competition.

Dharma is the state where we embody forgiveness and compassion for all beings, regardless of what they have done. By embracing this energy, we can live more joyfully. Even when facing individuals who have wronged us, our thoughts towards them shift to understanding and empathy. This transformation allows for a deep integration within us, enabling us to move forward with honor in our interactions with each soul. We can even send love to those who have harbored darkness and caused destruction. As we align more closely with dharma, we can reduce the karmic lessons we encounter. Otherwise, being stuck in the karmic wheel feels like cycling endlessly with a metaphorical "kick me" sign on our backs. Recognizing each lesson, enveloping it in love, doing the necessary introspective work, and releasing it is all part of the journey.

My Recent Example of Figuring Out a Love Triangle that was Exposed in this Life

Some examples of these relationships:

- In a tumultuous love affair, frequent arguments, breakups, and reconciliations bring out the best and worst in each other.
- Sibling rivalry leads to a constant sense of competition.
- Longing for love and affection from an abusive parent creates a challenging emotional dynamic.
- Both partners struggle for control in a marriage, leading to power struggles. Dealing with infidelity or exploitation

from a significant other adds further complexity. This may be a relationship where the romance or friendship has dwindled, but you fear leaving to learn the next lesson.

- Feelings of jealousy and ongoing power struggles mar a friendship.
- A colleague or boss at work is abusive, and you need to learn how to find your boundaries and seniority.

Use your rose or gauge to ask questions to see if a person is a soulmate.

1. When you met them, it felt like time slowed down.
2. A twin flame can also be a soulmate. Look for similar physical traits like eyes, hands, and birthmarks.
3. Do you get flashes of another life or time, or a feeling of a different space and time when you were together? Those are real; you should believe them, write them down, and keep track of these images.
4. When you meet them, it seems like you already know them. This will feel different than a twin flame; it will feel like you are floating and buzzing with intense energy in your back, stomach, or forehead.
5. You go deep into each other's life fast.
6. There were synchronicities that you can reflect on that were pulling you together.
7. They awaken something in you that you have not felt before or haven't felt in a long time.
8. You get a sense that they are in your life for a reason.
9. If they have a trait that you need to learn, write it down. They might be there to teach you something, like a colleague, a boss, or a financial advisor, and you know they have something for you. Pay attention to the energy and the signs.

Please use your rose and gauge to ask questions and get answers.

____

____

____

____

Week 5. Day 3 – Soul/Karmic Storylines – Exercise

Meditation. We can choose which meditation you want, but at least do The Liberated Healer's Zipper Energy Meditation, Grounding Meditation, or the other calming meditations given as options for you (20 minutes minimum before this work).

Working on Karmic Relationships to Create a Better Life Here and Beyond

How are you wired to recognize a karmic connection? Can you list the people you feel have come in for significant lessons and what you learned?

____

____

____

____

Can you make decisions quickly, or do you get stuck and worried about everyone else's thoughts?

____

____

In group situations, do you take control? Are you around those who take control? If so, please list them here.

____

____

____

____

____

Are you someone who can think on their feet and come up with clever responses in conversations? Do your friends or coworkers appreciate and understand your sense of humor? You typically share a strong bond with these people, whether they are current connections or people from your past. Feel free to share some of these significant relationships, even if they are no longer actively in your life.

____

____

____

Do you have complete faith in yourself? Do you surround yourself with individuals who also have unwavering belief in themselves? People with similar mindsets tend to gravitate towards each other, and the saying "birds of a feather flock together" holds. If you seek to raise your own standards and energy levels, connecting with people who demonstrate the behaviors and attitudes you aspire to have for yourself is essential. Take a moment to identify some of these individuals below.

____

____

____

____

Do you have a strong will? Please do the same as above: list the people in your life who represent this and what they have done to display it.

____

____

____

____

Are you comfortable being the center of attention? Please list why you like this and others that seem the same.

____

Are you aware of what you do or don't like? Are you around others who are aware of themselves in this way? How does it feel to be around this confidence?

Are you able to be assertive when necessary? Are you around others who can be this way too? Is there something you like or don't like about this expression?

Are you good at asserting and reaching goals? Are you around others who are the same? List some of these goals here.

Are you good at self-restraint? Do you often exercise self-restraint? Are you around others who do this? Where can you add more self-restraint?

Are you confident when trying new things? Are you around others who are good at this? What do you like about this energy? How can you embody it more?

Are you highly motivated and not a procrastinator? Are you around other highly motivated people? Note anything that this brings up for you here. You will be working on these things to build the life you prefer.

The following section discusses the significance of certain character traits in our lives and their role in our personal development. It emphasizes the importance of self-awareness and the impact of these traits on our journey to success and fulfillment.

Week 5. Day 4 – Spiritual Teachers, God Light/Supreme Being/Source (Requests/ Prayers), Disco Ball of Protection

Love is not just a word but a movement and an action.
Meditation. We can choose which meditation you want, but at least do The Liberated Healer's Zipper Energy Meditation, Grounding Meditation, or the other calming meditations given as options for you (20 minutes minimum before this work).

Spiritual/Soul Teachers/Physical Guides
The people who come into our lives to teach essential lessons can take many forms. They might be someone close to us, like a sibling or a friend, or they could be a formal teacher, a colleague, or a spiritual mentor such as a shaman, guru, or priest. These individuals are trained and knowledgeable about spiritual matters and can guide us. However, once we've learned what we need from these teachers, it's important to integrate those lessons and sometimes even move on from the relationship, especially with a spiritual teacher. Knowing when to move on is

a valuable gift, not a sign of abandonment or negativity. A good spiritual teacher will understand this and not be upset if you choose to part ways.

If a teacher reacts negatively to your decision to leave or doesn't understand why you no longer want to work with them, it may be a sign that they weren't the right teacher for you. This realization could even be a lesson. Similarly, if a client doesn't return for more healing after a session, it does not reflect the healer's ability. It simply means that the client and the healer didn't resonate or needed more time to prepare for the lessons they were meant to learn. There's no judgment in these situations.

It's crucial to listen to your inner guidance when it comes to spiritual teachers who insist you stay in their programs or treatments. A genuine teacher will respect your intuition and free will. It could be a red flag if someone pressures you into expensive or indefinite commitments. There are also manipulative spiritual or religious groups that use fear to keep people from leaving, but these organizations are not aligned with positive intentions. You can test a teacher's authenticity by expressing your need for a break and observing their reaction. It's important to protect your energy and remove its influence from your life if it's negative.

God's Light/Supreme Being/Source (Requests/Prayers)

Prayers and rituals work as intentions for the light or the dark, depending on what you want to create on Earth. We detailed this in the section about light and dark energy. Anytime, pray from the heart; there is no wrong or right way. It's the energy and the intention behind what you are praying for, and it should be for good in this work we are doing. Don't pray for another to get hurt, something taken from them, or more. This is where you will surely build karma if you do those kinds of activities. When you go deeper like we are now, there needs to be an intention set and the need to call in extra protection and help.

Figure out how you would like to reference the light and how you connect to it. There is no correct answer for everyone, and this is very personal. As we move forward, you need this extra connection layer and protection. You have your protection rose, the glass body to protect you from others' energy. This will connect you to the light and more protection as we move through wounds, Akashic Records, and more!

I use all three of these names and change them out whenever I want, and spirit knows what I intend here.

Simple Exercise: Anytime you want to connect to the source of the light, imagine a bright, thick gold line or rope from your heart (Heart Chakra) and send it up to the heavens.

Say to yourself or out loud, *"Please connect me to the Supreme Being."*

You are connected. The energy needs to know you are asking for a direction connection. You can also add anything here, specifically a request or prayer. Here is a recommended prayer to open with any significant work you do moving forward.

I allow the Cosmic and Earth energies to flow through our bodies, opening the doors through which we become more aware of our spirituality and increase our communication with the God of our Heart.

Let us pray: *"May it be with the blessings of the Supreme Being (or how you connect with spirit) that whatever happens during this reading and healing will benefit us in our spiritual growth, awareness, understanding, and amusement. Amen."*

Mantras/Prayer

In a previous discussion, we highlighted the interconnectedness and sacredness of your words, thoughts, and actions with universal energy. It is crucial to prioritize your spiritual well-being, especially during times of disconnection, depression, or significant life changes. Discover practices that resonate with you, whether it's self-reflection, seeking strength and guidance, or manifesting positive outcomes through prayer. Your intentions have the power to shape your reality. Engaging in these practices elevates your spiritual frequency, causing lower vibrational energies to release their hold on you. Relationships that no longer align with your growth may naturally dissolve as you evolve. Appreciating these connections for the lessons they imparted and expressing gratitude for the growth they facilitated is essential. Doing so can create a positive path forward for yourself and those who have been part of your journey.

Everything is sacred if you call it so; everything is love if you call it so, so why don't we do it more? Shout it at the mountain tops or on a wave – whatever is in your heart!

Disco Ball of Light

Visualize yourself enclosed within a glittering disco ball emanating powerful gold and white light. As you ground yourself, visualize any lower vibrational energy being drawn into the center of the Earth. Envision the mirrors on the disco ball reflecting and repelling this energy, providing additional protection.

This extra protective visualization is beneficial when delving into deeper layers of energy work involving various energies that may be present in my surroundings. It's like adding a shield to ensure I don't carry unnecessary energy afterward!

Looking at Teachers' and Karmic Relationships' Purpose

Ensure you are grounded and have run your energy first to get the best readings. Please use your rose and gauge to ask questions and get answers.

What is the energy of this person concerning me? How does the rose look? Is it open or closed? What is the color?

Is this person trying to control my energy, and how much between 0–100?

Should I work with this person in my spiritual journey?

Is this person a soulmate, a teacher?

Just keep asking any questions you have and blow miniature roses on those roses or gauges so you can blow the energy no matter your answer. If they have come into your life, it is either to learn a lesson or to move into the future with them. This takes practice, but it's a fun and creative way to take control of all the relationships and situations in your life.

____

____

____

____

Week 5. Day 5 – Wound Work

Meditation. We can choose which meditation you want, but at least do The Liberated Healer's Zipper Energy Meditation, Grounding Meditation, or the other calming meditations given as options for you (20 minutes minimum before this work).

Clearing the Wounds and Storylines

Our stories and traumas shape our lives, affecting everyone to some extent. It can be challenging to keep this in mind when we feel stuck, and our experiences limit our perspective. The feeling that others have it easier often lingers in the background, creating a real struggle with comparison. I grapple with this frequently despite actively working to make my desired life. Even in my mid-50s, there are significant things I long for that still seem out of reach. Despite the doubts that creep in, I press on, and new opportunities emerge when I return to work. It's comforting to remind myself that everyone faces similar challenges at some point. I truly empathize with this struggle and wish it didn't have to be this way, shaped by our minds and experiences.

How to move forward: Integrate the healing and reflection and continue to work on this no matter how long it takes. Find places and people that make you feel safe to do the work.

Now, you should understand so much more about what a vast being and creature you are, and this helps to see that it is not just what is here today in the physical for you. This gives you a license to expand and recognize every critical interaction, person, job, and connection point you have ever created and why they are there. It should take out a little of the sense of loss or being lost, knowing that we are not only a part of this network, but our existence in it and how we vibrate is a vital source of energy contribution. You matter so much more than you ever knew, and you have right inside of you a vibration of pure Source, love, and the very thing that needs your help, and that is humanity.

Let's list some recurring storylines you have seen in this life. For me, it was suicidal ideation, illnesses that were said to be incurable, abusive family, partners, and even colleagues. If you start getting triggered during this exercise, move away from it and return when you are feeling up for this expression.

***We only typically have a handful of core wounds, three or four tops for each person.**

Storylines in my life that I recognize are patterns I want to work on and change.

I want to heal the Wounds I recognize in my life (not looking at what created them), just what they are now. For example, "I have an abandonment wound because my father left me as a child, which created a skewed relationship with the men in my life."

Even though these are listed here, it is not intended to dive into them all in one day. Pick one that you want and need to work on first. You will go back to this section to continue to work on these things for the rest of the program.

Exercise One: Once in a quiet environment and an excellent meditative space, let's pull up that first wound you feel is on repeat. Add your protection and prayers to open the session.

Please pull up a rose that represents this wound and look at it. Blow tiny roses on the rose to blow the energy that seems the same as the big rose you see. Listen to your intuition and gifts to get more answers. Ground that rose to the center of the Earth. Give that rose a Golden Sun. Keep blowing the roses. What are you seeing, feeling, hearing, or knowing? Take note. Are you seeing a person's face, an image? Are you feeling it in your body? Are you getting hot or cold? Everything tries to help you tell the story and look at the energy.

Keep blowing the tiny roses on top of the rose. You can also give yourself a Golden Sun to recall some energy back into you. Go gentle. Drop that rose when you feel ready.

Pull up a new rose and ask, *"What was this wound's purpose in my life?"*

For example, I was not able to have children in this lifetime and had many female issues. This was not in the cards for me, and it was very traumatic and sad. Through my work in energy, I finally got my answer, "I needed to learn how to mother myself in this life." Did it help me learn this? Yes. One, because I have been a mother several times, in several lives, and although I want this in the here and the now, it does not mean that I have not been a mother. This has been a core lesson and wound, and now I know about it, I can work hard to understand it more deeply. When it comes up and makes me sad or feel insignificant, I can hold myself in kind words and be gentle with myself. I am my own best friend. I want to survive, thrive, and get through these things to be as liberated as possible.

What relationships did this wound affect other than me?

____

____

____

____

What was the secondary effect created by this primary wound? For example, I was abandoned because my parents did not make me feel safe and left me alone a lot. The secondary effect was that I felt unworthy of love.

____

____

____

What do you feel, hear, know, or see when you blow these roses, anything in your body, and where? Write them down.

When examining this wound, please note if you observe any specific colors or images linked to it. Jot down these details, and if necessary, refer to the color chart to understand the significance of these colors. For instance, if you perceive a dark navy-blue hue in the wound, it may symbolize a controlling masculine energy. Similarly, a muted pink shade might indicate a controlling feminine energy akin to a grandmother.

____

____

____

____

____

Exercise Two for Wound Healing: Take a moment to center yourself and visualize bringing positivity and high vibrational energy into your space by connecting to the Supreme Being, giving yourself a Golden Sun, and giving yourself back as much energy as possible. Imagine gathering all your life force energy and a rainbow of uplifting energy around you. Repeat this visualization a few times, staying grounded in the present moment. Doing so can release any low vibrational energy lingering within you. Envision this energy flowing through you and visualize the transformative process, ensuring only positive and high vibrational energy enters your space.

ADD IN an Image of the Energy Flowing

Return to the color chart and see what color would help you. For example, you feel out of your power and want strength and confidence around these situations. If that is the case, please drop that old rose, pull up a new one, and look at the energy of that wound. It might be a muted color like purple, green, or yellow. Color flush that rose with bright, high vibrations, starting with "yellow" to regain your power. If you want to use the gauge to see where you are, ask it questions.

How much of this wound is in my personal space, 0–100? You might get a read in the high category, such as 80%. Keep blowing the roses, color flushing, and grounding.

This is a process, and it will get easier over time. Here are the phases of healing.

1. The Story: Shattered self and confusion, breaking down the wound so you can heal it.
2. The Causes and Conditions: Withdrawing the energy from inside/out and feeling the transformation.
3. The Soul Truth: Healing, Forgiveness, Understanding.

Whenever you feel overwhelmed, take a moment to ground yourself and run your Earth and Cosmic energy, asking your guides and connecting with the gold line up to the Supreme Being to come in and give you a Golden Sun. It's perfectly okay to take a break and return to this practice when ready. Remember, healing from past wounds is a journey that takes time, so there's no rush. There is no judgment here – only admiration for your commitment to this healing journey. You are capable of it. The first step may feel challenging because it delves deep, but it becomes easier as you go through the process. Each wound is unique, just as we all are. Keep persevering, for this is something within your reach. You can heal these wounds and replace them with love and joy. Although there may be a spiritual scar, it will remind you of the lessons learned and the strength you have gained.

Week 5. Day 6 – Illness Contracts/Exercises/ TV Screen Reading/Closing a Reading

Meditation. We can choose which meditation you want, but at least do The Liberated Healer's Zipper Energy Meditation, Grounding Meditation, or the other calming meditations given as options for you (20 minutes minimum before this work).

It's important to remember that the information provided here does not serve as a substitute for professional medical advice. Instead, it discusses spiritual contracts and how they may contribute to our well-being. When dealing with an illness, it's crucial to consider various sources of information and guidance to make the best decisions for our health. Ultimately, spiritual healing can offer valuable support for those living with a condition that affects their quality of life.

Contracts for Illness in this Life

To truly understand and embrace your essence, it's important to tune into the different energies and perspectives that make up your being. Each encounter with illness can provide new insights and tests. Today, we often confine ourselves to various rules, expectations, and social norms, making it challenging to live authentically and freely. It's about reaching a point where we genuinely feel at home in our bodies, minds, and souls rather than just intellectually acknowledging it.

As we journey through life, we work through our own karmic experiences and contribute to the collective karma of our loved ones and humanity. There are incredibly high-vibrational beings, perhaps even Earth Angels, who may willingly take on the burden of a profoundly debilitating and rare disease, knowing that their life will be filled with immense suffering. Do we express gratitude to these individuals for shouldering this tremendous burden on behalf of all of us? Perhaps less often than we should. These extraordinary souls possess an inner strength beyond comprehension, bravely enduring their struggles while wearing a smile on the outside despite the tremendous pain they harbor within. Their resilience inspires us all, reminding us to cherish and be grateful for the lives we have been blessed with. Let's take a moment to express our heartfelt appreciation for these remarkable individuals. We have heard their stories, and we know who they are. Some spend their entire lives confined to their beds, never tasting the freedom of the outdoors, the exhilaration of running, the joy of rolling in the grass, or the simple delight of playing with a puppy.

Spirit Giving You a Nudge

We all need spiritual hygiene and alchemy. An individual I recently met was initially diagnosed with stage 4 cancer and given a year to live. This life-altering news prompted him to reevaluate his connections and explore spirituality more deeply. He discovered that many of his relationships were superficial and that the support he expected was not readily available. After undergoing a tremendous shift in perspective, he received a call from his doctor informing him that his tests had been mixed up and he did not have cancer after all. This unexpected event prompted him to question how to return to his previous life after gaining such profound insights. He is now in the process of redefining himself and forging more meaningful connections, having been given a unique opportunity to reassess his life and deepen his spiritual journey, thereby building more profound relationships. What a gift from the spirit to give him a little shake of the trees to let the leaves fall out, and in his case, he didn't get the disease that was going to be devastating for his body, body, spirit, and soul.

Spiritual Alchemy

Many of you have the power to transmute your illnesses. This passage talks about the power of transformation and the ability to shift one's reality, particularly about illness and genetic conditions. It discusses the concept of transmutation, where individuals have the potential to change their genetic codes and DNA through spiritual alchemy, ultimately altering the frequency of their experience from dark to light. It suggests that illnesses often have underlying emotional roots and that individuals may have chosen specific experiences in their lives, such as Down syndrome, for their soul's growth. The passage also acknowledges the challenge of transmutation for some genetic conditions and suggests that it can be a familial experience.

Use this image to activate St. Germain in your space.

Using St. Germain to Help Transform an Illness. This is your instruction for a spiritual alchemy ritual to transform low frequencies associated with diseases and illnesses into love within the body. **This exercise will take 30-45 minutes.**

There is a process of shifting one's perspective. For example, if someone has Lupus, they might initially perceive it as a complex and dangerous illness. However, their perspective changes through the spiritual alchemy ritual, and they start seeing the energy as love rather than something destructive. This change in perspective can help stop the blocking of chakras and alleviate symptoms.

Suppose you get emotional stress triggers, or your cellular memory gets activated. In that case, your symptoms might temporarily reappear, but conducting the spiritual alchemy ritual again can help transmute them back to love. The physical body may need time to adjust to the process of transmutation, and discomfort may be felt initially as the body pushes the energy through each meridian. Overall, this is an excellent additional tool to add to one's healing journey.

The ritual is not a replacement for medical treatment but rather an extra tool to aid in healing and transmuting lower frequencies. It also discusses the potential emotional triggers and cellular memories associated with illnesses and how they can be addressed through further spiritual alchemy to bring them back to love. This ritualistic approach to healing and transmutation highlights the belief in the power of conscious intention and spiritual connection in addressing health challenges.

- Get into a meditative state. Light candles—if you have violet ones, that's even better!
- Use the color flushing technique and flush all of you with the brightest violet you can imagine. This is a very potent color and is the primary color St. Germain uses when healing to change the physical, mental, emotional, and spiritual body.
- Invite St. Germain to come into your space and ask, "May I please have a healing?"
- Write down the names of the diseases and infections on paper, holding the paper in your hands and invoking St. Germain while commanding the violet flame to evolve within your conscience. The words and letters on the paper are believed to contain light code frequencies that can transmute the lower frequency back to love within the disease or illness.

- Be present in the moment and call upon a higher power or divine source to transmute the illness back to perfect health. Say or pray, "I command these illnesses to be transmuted back to love."
- Continue the ritual even if it feels ineffective initially, as it may take time for the physical body to adjust to the transmuted frequencies.

Mental Health Healing

Aside from the spiritual work on mental health healing, here are a few other recommendations to implement.

Commitment to healing what is going on, gently and with kindness. Everyone has something; this is your something — we can do this together. Understanding the illness from many sides will help you know what is happening. There will be ebbs and flows, but others have been able to reduce and even heal their mental health conditions, and so can you or anyone you love.

Safety Plan. If you have any fears about what you can or might do to yourself or if you know anyone suffering, please create a simple safety plan (in this chapter). Even if you don't share it with anyone (although sharing it is best practice and makes it even more effective), writing this out will help you connect to yourself. It also helps increase the likelihood that you will use the necessary steps to stay safe when it is more challenging to think under extreme distress.

Evaluate your Environment and make small changes (or even big ones if needed) that help you reduce stressors while prioritizing yourself. Entrust a supportive friend, family member, or professional to communicate how to calm your space or activities to reduce conflicts or anxiety around you.

Identify your level of self-love, realizing that it might need to increase exponentially, and try not to judge yourself for why it might be low, as many people do. Practicing self-love starts today; how you speak to yourself and carry yourself, even in the smallest of ways, will significantly help liberate you from the thoughts that take you over at times.

Patience is needed in all healing. When you have a negative moment or day, realize that this will pass, and you will have new energy tomorrow. Giving the emotions and situations room to breathe is also needed.

You have Committed to yourself, which is beautiful.

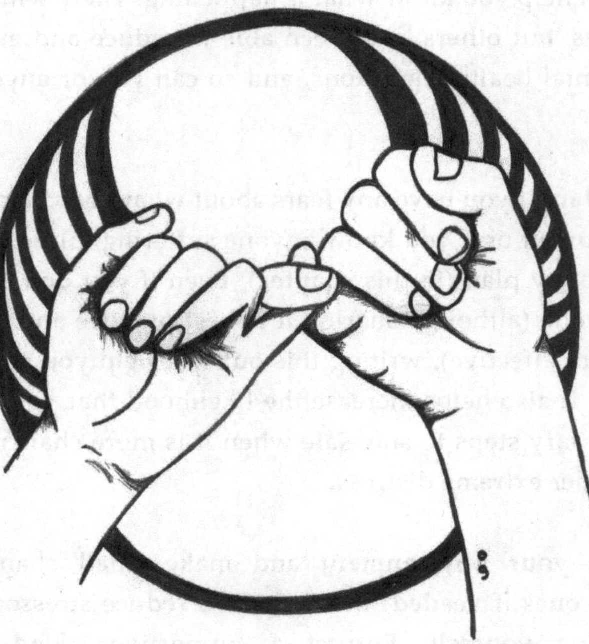

Relationship Healing

Meditation. We can choose which meditation you want, but at least do The Liberated Healer's Zipper Energy Meditation, Grounding Meditation, or the other calming meditations given as options for you (20 minutes minimum before this work).

Navigating through this process can be challenging as it involves unraveling the emotional and mental ties we have with the relationships in our lives. It may take a toll on a person's well-being. Even though it's beneficial regardless of the circumstances, it's essential to acknowledge that it will be an arduous journey. However, you will experience a sense of relief afterward, and the relationship dynamics will transform. You should feel much lighter once it's all resolved. Given the personal nature of this journey, it's common for healers or energy workers to seek assistance from others because of its difficulty. If you struggle through this, please know your struggles are acknowledged and empathized.

Only do one person at a time and on the same day; do not mix the energies in one day.

Meditation. Feel calm and ready to go into this space.

Ask them first. It's best to mention or ask them if you can do a healing. If you have done one of them in the past and they permitted you to do so, then you can. If not, all you can do is run their energy.

Call them into the session. Have a chair or a place where you will ask them to sit. We do this by saying, "Hello (and then their name three times)." Do it repeatedly until you feel the energy shift and they are sitting before you. This will be just a part of their spirit engaging with you. Tell them, "I want to work on the energy in our relationship."

Run their energy. Ground them, run their Earth and cosmic Energy, give them a Golden Sun and a protection rose, and hook them up to the Supreme Being.

Pull up a rose that represents your relationship. Place it between the two of you in the center and look at the rose. What colors are in there? Are they muted or dark? You must blow the roses to transmute the energy if the roses are not bright.

Blow roses. Take miniature roses that look the same color as the rose you see and blow them onto the rose as much as possible. Ground the rose to the center of the Earth and surround the rose with love. You can say things to the rose that represent how you are feeling. Talk to the rose and say what you struggle to tell the person. They will get the energy and the information. Always do it with kindness and love. If you put in negative or revengeful energy, it will backfire back to you. This is a holy, peaceful, generous act because you care about that person. Love, laughter, light, and friendship are only allowed here.

Drop the rose. Pull up another rose. Look at the new rose and see what has changed. You might have to do this a few times until you break the energy. You might get visions and write them down. They are communications between you. A past life image might come up, a blockage feeling like anger. Have some awareness so you know what to work on.

Pendulum. Use the pendulum if you need a specific answer.

Move. Play crystal bowls, sing, or play the drums—whatever you need to move the energy. You can even get up and dance with your partner, friend, or family member. By breaking up the stuck energy, you are healing each other again in kindness and love.

Drop everything. You can use the gauges from 0 to 100 if you need more information. When you feel like you have moved enough energy, you should give it a break for now.

Run new energy. Recall your life force energy from that person to give both of you new energy, grounding, and Golden Suns.

Thank them. Be kind and grateful for doing the work together, and let them return in their way.

Make sure you close out the session and give yourself new energy. Please note whether they texted you while you were doing this work. I am sure they were thinking of you and wondering why you were suddenly so top of mind for them. This is a positive way to work on any relationship on your own. What a great tool. You can do something good for everyone by yourself. Once you can do this and get through it, you will use this a lot for many people you feel stuck with and want to continue having them in your life.

My Safety Plan

This Is Me, and I Am Here.

Name: ______________________________

What are at least three warning signs that I am in crisis (thoughts, feelings, moods, situations, behavior)?

1. ______________________________

2. ______________________________

3. ______________________________

What are at least three internal coping strategies (e.g., meditation, chanting, positive thinking, and grounding skills like counting) I can use?

1. ______________________________

2. ______________________________

3. ______________________________

What are at least three external coping strategies (e.g., dancing, running, taking a bath) I can use?

1. ______________________________

2. ______________________________

3. ______________________________

What items should I keep out of my environment to ensure safety (e.g., alcohol, guns, prescription medications)?

1. ______________________________

2. ______________________________

3. ______________________________

What can I add to my environment to increase safety (e.g., candles, photos of a loved one, inspirational quotes)?

1. ______________________________

2. ______________________________

3. ______________________________

What are at least three social spaces I consider safe that I can go to?

1. ______________________________

2. ______________________________

3. ______________________________

People I can ask for help:

Name ______________ Phone ______________
Name ______________ Phone ______________
Name ______________ Phone ______________

In the case of a crisis, the professionals or agencies to contact are:

Therapist or clinician ______________ Phone ______________
Guardian or emergency contact ______________ Phone ______________
Local emergency service ______________ Phone ______________

Rose or Pendulum Work for Mental Health

Meditation. We can choose which meditation you want, but at least do The Liberated Healer's Zipper Energy Meditation, Grounding Meditation, or the other calming meditations given as options for you (20 minutes minimum before this work).

As you lie down, you can use a Pendulum to scan your body and identify areas where energy might be stuck. This stuck energy can stem from mental, physical, or emotional wounds that affect your aura and contribute to various mental health issues. By observing the pendulum's movements and asking it specific questions as it hovers over different parts of your body, you can gain insights into addressing and healing these wounds. It's an intriguing process that can uncover layers of mental health issues and other stories you may be carrying. Once you determine where the stuck energy resides, revisit the St. Germain practice for that specific area or move on to the rosework technique.

Pull up a rose and ask your questions about where your mental health is stuck inside of you. You can image your body from head to toe in a rose if you want and scan from top-down and look for the colors:

- MUTED YELLOW – Mental Health Issues
- MUTED GREEN – Physical Health Issues
- MUTED RED – Emotional Issues
- MUTED PURPLE – Spiritual Issues

New Exercise to Look at the Whole Body – TV Screen Scanner

Meditation. We can choose which meditation you want, but at least do The Liberated Healer's Zipper Energy Meditation, Grounding Meditation, or the other calming meditations given as options for you (20 minutes minimum before this work).

Turn your crown chakra golden as you read your entire energy body. Imagine a giant TV screen out in front of you, and it is blank. Ground the TV screen to the center of the Earth. Imagine your entire body inside of the screen. Blow tiny little roses on the screen to start to read the energy.

*If you are reading another person's energy, you need to get their permission first, then go back to the way you were taught to read by saying the opening prayer, saying their name three times, and making sure you have your protection up!

Look for the colors above and ask questions. Where do I have muted yellow in my space? Continue down the colors. Note what you are seeing. Continue to blow the miniature roses in the area that you visit. Give yourself a Golden Sun to recall all the energy from this issue. Then, surround that area with violet light and ask the Supreme Being or St. Germain to clear the energy. Do this until the energy is looking better and a more vibrant color. You can even use the gauge to learn precisely where you are regarding the percentage of work you need to do. Once you identify the areas needing healing, you should do this often until you can get to a clear, high vibrational color.

Close the Readings (a revisit)

You are gaining more tools, and now you must learn how to close a reading quickly.

Close out the reading. If you are reading someone else, you can let them go; if not, you must close this process.

Imagine a giant old book opening. Write the name of the person in the book, and imagine all the images, thoughts, and anything from the reading/healing being put inside the book. Close the book and say in your head or aloud, *"End of healing, end of reading, end of communication."*

Ground and Golden Sun. Drop your grounding cord and give yourself a new one and a final sizeable Golden Sun.

Week 5. Day 7 – Integration and Look at What We Have Learned Thus Far

Today, we'd like you to review the list below and revisit the things you are still challenged with or want to get more clarity on and practice, practice, practice. We know this takes time, so it is called *A Handbook for the Living*. Living is not just a moment; it's many moments, and it will all start to fall into place soon. You will begin to see how it is positively affecting your life. When an event takes you into an unfavorable space, you can use these tools to pull you out! You have so many tools in your toolkit! Hello expert!

Take a moment to reflect on your journey and acknowledge your progress. This is a time to celebrate your personal growth and development. Your guides, angels, and elementals cheer you on as you embrace love and expansion. Have you noticed the increase in self-love within you each day? Do you recognize how the universe influences your emotions and appreciate the complexity and beauty of your soul's journey? Each person you encounter plays a role in your growth, helping you become the master of your path. You carry the divine essence, a spark of light that connects you to the greater purpose of existence. Exploring the profound question of our existence and understanding our place in the universe is essential.

Can we all try to come together in a spirit of love and unity, holding onto that positive energy even toward those with whom we may have conflicts, such as those with whom we may have conflicts in various aspects of life, such as politics, race, social status, karmic connections, and the individuals we tend to judge and criticize? Today, let's strive for inner peace encompassing our entire being — body, mind, spirit, and soul.

Grounding (Self, Vehicles, Locations, Projects, Objects, Animals, the Planet)
Earth & Cosmic (Connecting us to the Universe — Running our entire Energy Grid)

Golden Suns (Recalling our Life Force Energy back into our space)

Center of Your Head (You should be the only one in your head, moving everyone else out)

Rosework (How to read energy)

Present-Time (Being here today so you can do the work – not in the past or the future)

Blowing Roses (How to transmute the energy)

Protection Rose (Using a rose alongside your Aura to protect your energy)

Body of Glass (Extra protection where energy slides off you)

Learning Your Gifts (Chosen life gifts specific to you)

Learning Your Themes (Chosen life themes specific to you)

Disco Ball Protection (You are inside the ball with light and mirrors bounding energy away from you)

Color Flushing (Knowing colors so you can transmute them into more of what you want)

Chakra Work (Understanding your energy centers)

Reading Yourself and Another Person (The setup and how to complete a session)

Opening a Reading (The ritual or prayer and intention for what you are doing)

Closing a Reading (The closing of the energy so it can stop flowing and be archived)

Zipper Meditation (Zipping in good energy for the day and zipping out to get refreshed at the end of the day)

Karma versus Dharma Rosework (Getting through the karma in your life)

Ho'oponopono Meditation (Forgiveness for self and others meditation)

Pendulum Work (To read the energy and get your questions answered)

Mock-up Manifestations (How to set the energy and call in what you want)

Rosework (For Twin Flames, Soulmates, and more)
Guides (Connection with your masters, angels, and guides)
Meditations (Rainbow In – Fire Out, and Gold In – Silver Out)
Energy Gauge (Using 00–100 to determine the percentage of energy in your or others' space)

The New Monk – Week 6 – Inner Child Work/Death/Passing/ Life Review/Humanity

The New Monk (You) Where You Can See in Many Directions of Your New Life.

"Dark is the Oil. Light is the Water ... some particles will not connect."

We are all spiritual, no man over another. Yes, we have teachers

Thus, students, we all have a spiritual birthright, and here we are!

Week 6. Day 1 – Inner Child Work

A call to love is needed.
Go to the child in your heart.
Do you love that child?
If yes, then bring that to the forefront.
If you don't, ask that love to get louder so you can hear it again!

Inner Child Healing

We can trace back many things we all want and need to heal to our childhood, for all souls. I've never seen a person not have childhood wounds, no matter what their station in life. For example, even if you came from and had excellent parental relations, you might have had a bully at school, or a family member taunt you, or fears of being an empath or an illness. Because so many, and maybe all people, can relate to some childhood wound, that is where we must go. It's later because you need to practice many of the tools we listed in the last chapter to prepare yourself, mostly in honor of and to support you. Not to put you in fear, but so you can feel more confident going into this space because many of us will get triggered. This is a delicate matter and not to be taken lightly. Hold yourself as this book and the intention behind it holds you. But once there is a release, even though it was so delicate, there will be a soft, warm, and loving energy that covers you, your self-love, and the divine, giving you a well-earned slap on the back and saying, "Good job!"

I've had profound healing with my suicidal ideation and illnesses through this very last part of my primary education through the teaching in this *Handbook for the Living*. I had severe childhood wounds, so it was easy for me to know where I had to go, but I couldn't jump right in because I was in utter fear of getting to my core wounding. I did this last bit where I felt safer and healthier. If you are not ready for this, skip it and return to it anytime. Invite people to hold space for you if needed; you must be your advocate and know what you need and when. Return to meditations like Ho'oponopono, which will help you relax in this work. We got this; we got you! You are strong like a lion.

Inner Child Connections

This is deep, profound healing. However, whether you see your inner child as a female, male, or both is up to you. When we first dive into this process, the inner child usually hides. So, there will be an uncovering and practice of communicating. They know you want to connect with them and will feel you before they show themselves. If you create art, music, a business, or anything you want to make through your inner child, this is where we can.

The Practice

- **Visualize a guide that you can relate to to support you.** This can be Jesus, Buddha, an Angel, or one of the guides we listed in the previous chapters, or at least connect with a higher consciousness. You will feel the energy in your heart space. Have fun!
- **Go into Meditation.** Use the grounding practice and imagine tree roots coming from your feet this time. Call in a Golden Sun over your head and ask, "Please bring in my higher consciousness of healing." See, feel, hear, or know that this golden light is now traveling to your physical heart.
- **Visualize a safe place.** If you can, make this a place in nature or a crystal palace for yourself now or when you were a child, where you would have felt safe. This would be a place where no humans have or could ever hurt you; if you like animals, surround yourself with them, plants, a dome of light, a crystal palace, flowers, trees, or anything

that you know makes you feel secure, safe, warm, and understanding. No one can ever come into this place without their permission. Include a toy or anything that would resonate with that child. You can create anything you want that makes them safe.

- **Make the meeting.** See yourself in spirit (the version of you that you feel the most comfortable with), see this small child, make an introduction, and begin to ask questions. *"How old are you? Hello, I am you. I am all grown-up. I wasn't aware that you are in my heart; now that I know you are here, I will ask you for permission to do what you want. As a child, you did not get the respect you deserved; I am here to give it to you now. I love you, and I am sorry I hurt you. Please forgive me, and thank you. I am sorry I ignored you for many years. What do you need? You are in a safe place that I have created for you and surrounded you with* (insert the things you added above that will help them feel secure)."
- **Once comfortable, bring in the guide from above (Jesus, etc.).** They will guide your inner child into a light and show them that they have never been separated from God and that it has all been an illusion. As children, they felt all alone, but Christ's consciousness or Jesus was always with them. (Create your energy based on your belief system. If it's not Jesus, do not follow what is not proper to your heart.) This is the divine love you've been seeking.
- **Get permission from the inner child.** "Are you okay to proceed?" Check in on them constantly. Show them that this has all been a part of the ego game. That they have never been separated and again are never alone. Once you are in a good place and taken to the light, the guides will bring them back to your heart.
- **Work on this daily for a few days.** Do not bring anyone else into their safe place without their permission. Let

them have a voice for what they need; allow them to speak their truth. It is time for the inner child to be heard.

- **Anger might come out.** Children are often scolded and need to be given the actual ability to speak their minds or be heard. This is where they get to be expressive, so you might see some anger or swearing (even in life, this is often where this comes out in real life). The deep frustration of being stuck in the adult world, coupled with fear and the feeling of not being safe or able to connect authentically to their needs and wants. Pay attention to these things or even a pain in your body. If the inner child pulls on your coat to get your attention, these subtle energies are, "I need to show you who I am and how to love me."
- **Ask:** "How do I love you?" If you feel guilty at any time, bring in compassion for yourself. You need to get this before giving it to everyone else; why do you seek others to love and not yourself? Your connection to the divine is within; it is time to return to the heart. You will feel more love coming through.
- **Ego.** At first, your ego will try to tell you this is not working, but then you will start to feel it, and you will start to feel more joy.
- **Hug.** Come in and hold them in a way that is comfortable with you. Maybe you will rock them and tell them you are so sorry for what they went through. Look in their eyes and wipe their tears. Feel their heart as they are panicked, sad, or confused.
- **Release.** The first couple of times might feel like a big release, and you should let it happen if you are emotionally safe to do so. Let that pain and fear out. Remember, you have a grounding cord that allows this all to come out and burn away into the center of the Earth.
- **Call in Golden Suns.** Use any tool connected to you to ensure your Earth and Cosmic energies are running.

- **Do something fun.** Imagine getting up now, grabbing their hand, and doing something fun where you will laugh and go into the energy of amusement. This can be jumping into the ocean, swimming, roller skating, swinging from trees, playing with animals, or anything that breaks the energy and goes into kindergarten energy.
- **Kindergarten Energy.** This has been programmed out of our existence and is one of the keys to a happy life. It's the ability to keep your innocence and childlike spirit. Spirit never ages, our physical body does, our mind gains new information, and our emotional self expands, but why are we being taught that we can't have belly laughs every day? We can't fall in love when it arrives because there are too many rules; we can't have crushes on someone else where we must play games and are too afraid to express our care and love. This is such a big reason why our people on this planet are suffering. Let's go back now with permission from the inner child.
- **Ha-Ha-Ha – Amusement.** Again, laugh, and if you can't because you are crying too much, start saying, "Ha, Ha, Ha." Do it repeatedly because we need to fake it until we make it sometimes. Laugh with your inner child, smile wildly, without care, feel the breeze on your face or the smell of the ocean if that is where you are, and try to activate all your senses.
- **See Your Own Eyes.** Now, stare into your child's eyes, sending love to every chakra point from your adult self to your little self. See yourself filled with the colors from the chart, giving them new energy, and see their eyes lighten.
- **Heart-to-heart hug.** Let them know you will never leave them again, and give one last final big heart-to-heart hug and ask for any final guidance or words of wisdom your little self wants to tell you. Come back and visit them often, and you can explore many different healing

scenarios. Your guides will be there to help you and show you the way. By now, you have strengthened this muscle with practice and are more in control of your healing.

- **Say Goodbye.** Let your inner child return to a safe place for now, and let them know you will return. Tuck them in or whatever you think will make them happy.
- **Repeat the Steps.** Drop your old grounding cord and give yourself a new one. The final gold sounds recall your energy from this experience and rerun your Earth and Cosmic energy.
- **Journal.** Do you want to remember anything from this experience, or do you think you continue next time?

Please note your experiences and what your inner child did when you first saw them emerge from the shadows.

What did they look like? What were they wearing?

____

____

What did they say?

____

____

____

What safety items did you give them? Where was their safe place?

____

____

____

____

What do you want to take away from this moment?

____

____

____

____

With this intellect, many principles will be assimilated, and you'll bring various people, projects, and experiences into your new version of you that vibrate with your authentic being. You will feel like you are part of the world and better know how to unveil what is meant for you and why it is showing up.

As mentioned, make sure to take it easy on yourself. This is a big day for your entire being, and most of the work before has been to get you ready for this day, so please do something nice for yourself for the rest of the day, even if it's a walk, a bath, or something that is calming and gentle.

Week 6. Day 2 – Energy Archetypes

The most rewarding aspect of this work was gaining a deeper insight into the inevitable experience we will all face at some point — departing from our physical bodies. I am sure that I will not decide when my life ends. This is a statement I couldn't have made in the past, but it holds for me now.

If you are afraid of death, this message is for you. Understanding more about what happens after death can bring great relief to both the living and those who have lost loved ones.

In today's modern world, many of us are either driven to live life to the fullest or are held back by fear, preventing us from pursuing the adventures we desire. I'm reminded of Philippe Petit, the French high-wire artist who famously walked the tightrope between the Twin Towers in 1974 (*The Wire*, 2015). Despite knowing that death was ever-present during his daring act, he was driven by a profound awareness of the balance between embracing life and acknowledging mortality. This perspective seems lacking in our Western culture today. Why don't we see more people taking such extraordinary risks anymore? Our society has conditioned us to fear everything, making it easier to control. The relentless focus on things like credit scores subtly influences our lives, shaping our actions and decisions. It's as if we're constantly being told what to do, what to be, and how to act without considering spirituality. This pervasive influence leads to confusion, a lack of trust, and unresolved childhood wounds, leaving many feelings lost. Did you know that with just 3% of the world standing up against unjust systems like credit scores, we could change or eliminate them? Each of us holds more power than we realize; collectively, we are even more vital.

Acknowledging the reality of death is just one step in understanding the bigger picture of life. Every moment, whether good, bad, beautiful, ugly, scary, or sad, is a precious part of our journey. With the wealth of tools and information available, we should be eager to see how we handle different situations and recognize the patterns that no longer serve us. With the right tools, we can release these patterns and find calmness, understanding the energy behind our experiences and even exploring the concept of past lives triggering our current struggles.

Archetypes/Release that Old Ball and Chain

Understanding the spiritual archetypes that resonate with you is valuable for personal growth. These archetypes symbolize the various roles we assume along our spiritual journey. Each archetype represents a unique path toward spiritual enlightenment and embodies specific qualities associated with that path.

This exercise is particularly enlightening because it prompts introspection into our behavioral patterns without fear of shame, judgment, or criticism. I've recognized that I used to embody the victim archetype, continuously falling into that role without awareness. Although I genuinely experienced challenging events that made me a victim, I eventually began to wear that identity as a badge, intertwined with the fabric of my life. Once I acknowledged this pattern, I applied various processes I had learned to work through the associated energy, allowing me to move forward.

It's important to remember that we're constantly evolving through different archetypes. Although some individuals may have navigated past certain archetypes, it's an ongoing journey for most of us. This journey through archetypes adds depth and complexity to the profound game called Life! Some books label you as holding these for a lifetime; that is not how it has been shown to me. I no longer have the archetype of "victim" in my work, as this is the process.

There are thousands of archetypes, but here is the list we will focus on. I recommend using the pendulum to get quick, yes-or-no answers.

Spiritual Archetypes

These are self-explanatory about the traits that each might bring. Here is an example of the energy and how we might want to shift the energies that work for your life today or now.

Example. I feel anxious preparing to raise funds for the upcoming business meeting. I decided to use a pendulum or practice rosework to address this. Through this, I realize that I am in a state of "The Victim" or "The Child," which triggers fears about receiving the desired answer. I understand the need to shift this energy and move into a space of "The King" or "The Queen," embodying more power and seniority. This energy shift will better position me to receive the support and resources needed to achieve my goals. You will still have the other archetype energy, but it's not front and center.

The Achiever	The Innocent	The Pioneer
The Addict	The Jester	The Protector
The Advocate	The Judge	The Queen
The Alchemist	The King	The Rebel
The Angel	The Liberator	The Rescuer
The Artist	The Lover	The Ruler
The Caregiver	The Magical Child	The Saboteur
The Child	The Magician	The Sage
The Creator	The Maiden	The Self
The Empath	The Martyr	The Shadow
The Explorer	The Mediator	The Shaman
The Father	The Messenger	The Storyteller
The Guide	The Monk	The Victim
The Healer	The Mother	The Visionary
The Helper	The Mystic	The Warrior
The Hero	The Orphan	
The Huntress		

Spirituality Personality Type

Type 1: Reformer	Type 2: Helper	Type 3: Achiever
Type 4: Individualist	Type 5: Investigator	Type 6: Loyalist
Type 7: Enthusiast	Type 8: Challenger	Type 9: Peacemaker

Practice

Meditation. Please do The Liberated Healer grounding meditation, Earth & Cosmic, Golden Suns, and Protection for 20 minutes before this work. Here is what we are accomplishing:

- Identify the archetype within you currently.
- Work the energy and the root cause of the archetype.
- Death to that spiritual identity.
- Rebirth.

Pull up a gauge.

- Ask the spirit gauge to reveal to you, *"From 0 to 100, how much invalidation do I have in my space?"* There should be a good amount; we all have it. Say hello to that validation in your place; imagine it releasing down the grounding cord, creating and destroying some roses, and letting that release.
- Ask your spirit gauge, *"How much judgment and criticism are in my space, 0–100?"* They might be there because you are resisting something in your space. Don't be too serious; if you are feeling the weight of the energy, call in a Golden Sun filled with Amusement.
- Now, ask your spirit gauge, *"How much competition is in my space, from 0 to 100?"* Create and destroy some roses to release that energy.
- Say hello to your vibration of where you are right now, and make sure you are present.
- Now ask, are many people in your space giving you their opinion and giving you lots of input into who and what you are? You can ask, *"0–100, how many people are contributing to the amount of energy in my space?"* Create

and destroy roses to blow that energy and bring in some Golden Suns for a total energy refill.

- These archetypes are often unconscious aspects of ourselves that need to be reset so they can be in or out of our space correctly. We can keep internal patterns, but we want them to be positive.
- Pick one of the archetypes you want to work on and create a large rose in front of you that represents that archetype. Blow roses on the rose to help blow that energy. You can also use the gauge again to see how much of this energy is in your space and follow the tools to work this energy (Grounding, Present-Time, Golden Suns, Center of Your Head, Earth & Cosmic, Bring in Amusement, Creating and Destroying Roses). Say hello to this energy and create and destroy roses over the archetype. It will start to dissipate out of you.
- Pay attention to the images and things you see, feel, hear, know, and journal about. What are you releasing? Do you see people or a situation in your space? Are you yawning or sneezing? This is all energy!
- Continue to do this until you feel you have moved that energy out of your space. You control who you are and what you want to bring in. In this process, you will also release other people's energies into your space.
- You will feel distracted at times, too; that is an energy as well, and you can create and destroy roses to blow that energy.
- Now that the energy is gone or low, it is time to bring in the energy you want. We call this "Havingness." What energy do you want to have?
- Imagine a giant Golden Sun over your head, filling it with the archetype of energy you want to have now.
- Make one Golden Sun that is filled with *"Validation!"*

- What do we want? We want our pain to go away. We are afraid of going through other painful happenings and want to get to the REBIRTH and not have to process the EGO Death, but this is our first life's mission.

List any notes from these sessions:

____

____

____

____

Week 6. Day 3 – I Am Invocation – You are the Holy Grail You've Sought

This is an invocation by the ascended master, St. Germain. This is to protect and free all individuals who make a conscious effort to obtain mastery over all things on Planet Earth. Those who seek the health of their soul as humanity goes through a period of karmic generational chaos over the choices of humankind to keep them tethered to wars, abuse, rivalry in politics, and using money for power to control those lower than themselves. The individuals need this release and inner understanding of the "I am" presence. This is a conscious application of a mighty blessing. It will bring in intense love and let the perfection of this beautiful protection all around you. It will open the door of intelligence and help you manifest the life you prefer, which is charged with the consciousness of St. Germain. Forever self-sustained.

Activity: When you say and feel "I AM," you release the spring of eternal, everlasting life to flow unmolested and open the door to its natural flow wide. When you say, "I AM NOT, I CANNOT, I AM SICK, I AM BROKE," you close the door and bring that energy to you.

I AM: Recognize perfection in yourself; you know you are God and have all those that represent that in your life. Use these two words often. Anytime you are stuck, accept only the perfection in your life as I AM. Awaken to the fact that your thoughts and feelings have created everything in your world today. Learn to command the energy in your body. Please stand up and face the things you need to and overcome them. This brings you freedom. It would be best to do it yourself; nobody can do it for you. Here are some words you should consider using in your meditation.

Meditation. Please do The Liberated Healer grounding meditation, Earth & Cosmic, Golden Suns, and Protection for 20 minutes before this work. Put on calming music if that helps you to get into a great practice. Let it all flow through you.

Here are I AM ideas for you to shout aloud, sing, or in your mind. This will push out the low-vibrational energy that stops you from "Having the life you prefer."

I AM GOD
I AM HEALTHY (MIND, BODY, SPIRIT, AND SOUL)
I AM ABUNDANT
I AM FREE
I AM WHOLE
I AM LOVE
I AM LOVED
I AM INTELLIGENT IN MY BEING
I AM CONNECTED TO LIGHT
I AM THRIVING

I AM DOING
I AM WONDER
I AM EXPLORATION
I AM UNIQUE
I AM HAPPY
I AM BEING
I AM BEAUTIFUL
I AM STRONG
I AM CONFIDENT
I AM DIVINE
I AM WISE
I AM PRESENT
I AM AMUSED
I AM CREATIVE
I AM INTUITIVE
I AM PASSION
I AM THANKFUL

Week 6. Day 4 – Physical Death, Life Review, Your Original Soul Names

Meditation. Please do The Liberated Healer grounding meditation, Earth & Cosmic, Golden Suns, and Protection for 20 minutes before this work. Put on calming music if that helps you to get into a great practice. Let it all flow through you.

Many people today feel comfortable sharing their experiences of witnessing deaths or near-death experiences and the profound wisdom gained from these encounters. The freedom to express these experiences without fear of persecution is a testament to the progress of humanity. The stories shared are genuinely captivating. Hospice nurses, in particular, bear witness to numerous deaths, and some have even ventured into sharing their experiences on platforms like YouTube. One nurse recounted how she could sense when a person's time was near. The individuals would exhibit certain behaviors, such as looking upwards and communicating with unseen entities, shortly before passing away. According to her, this behavior indicated the presence of their soul family, angels, ancestors, and even animals waiting to guide them to the other side. Ensuring that the departing soul is attended to immediately is of utmost importance. As the time of passing approaches, our spiritual and soul knowledge becomes more pronounced and is put into practice. Understanding this care process brings comfort and tranquility to those who fear death and worry about the well-being of their loved ones. Moreover, this care extends to humans and embraces all living beings. Hence, it is unsurprising that many individuals who delve deeper into spiritual practices often adopt vegetarianism.

Note: Once the Etheric Cord is cut, there is no way to bring that soul back into the body except if it is done within minutes of passing through a trained native shaman from the land where the death occurs. These individuals are scarce but can jump into the spiritual world and do things no humans can.

Archangel Azrael, the Great Transitioner.

Archangel Azrael

In scary films, the Archangel Azrael is often depicted as the Grim Reaper, but his actual role is overseeing smaller groups of deaths. In situations involving large numbers of people passing away simultaneously, the highest order of angels — the Seraphim Angels — take charge. These powerful beings, with four faces representing the cardinal directions, are the only angels adorned in bright blue.

Our guardians and angels are always with us, offering comfort and support as we approach the end of our earthly journey.

When the time comes for the soul to leave the physical body, Azrael, the angel of death, appears with his scythe to sever the connection between the body and the soul. This connection is detached upon passing, except in cases where a child is born with a debilitating condition, maintaining a lifelong connection with their mother where they will have their etheric cord still attached. This mother will, unfortunately, feel a double detachment emotionally if she is still alive if this child passes during her life. The significance of this bond underscores the profound interconnectedness of life experiences.

The guides surround the person as the soul starts to ascend. If one could witness this transition, one would see the soul as a shimmering collection of golden stardust particles, initially scattered but gradually drawing together over about seven days. During this period, the soul recalls every life experience and gathers the energies it has shared with others, eventually becoming whole. This process, known as the "Life Review," brings an overwhelming sense of "Going Home" and an indescribable level of love and light. However, it takes a lot of work, especially for souls who have embraced the darker side of life in previous incarnations. There is a newer process for extremely dark souls that have been completely taken over, but these cases are sporadic. Hitler, for example, is said to have undergone a unique post-mortem experience to address the darkness within his soul. The complexities of his consciousness and energies will be explained in more detail soon.

Life Review – The movie of you

Upon leaving the body, the soul embarks on a profound life review guided by your spiritual team. The review encompasses the entirety of one's existence, starting from birth and unfolding like a movie. It swiftly traverses ordinary days while intermittently pausing for reflection. Throughout this process, one assumes the role of both spectator and participant, keenly experiencing the repercussions of one's actions on others. It's important to note that there is no judgment from the spiritual realm; individuals serve as their judges.

This review delves into even the minutest details, such as the impact of seemingly insignificant actions, like pulling a cat's tail as a toddler. Now, you must experience how it felt for the cat. It provides a comprehensive and objective overview of one's life, shedding light on the motivations behind both positive and negative choices. The process is not about judgment from external forces but rather a self-assessment. Moreover, it reveals how the cosmic forces have interwoven to narrate the individual's life story. The presence of spirits, guides, and angels during the individual's journey is also made apparent so you can plan for your next return to Earth (if you so choose – you will always have a choice, but you are seen as extremely brave for coming to Planet Earth).

The life review provides a higher perspective, transcending the limitations of human experience, and facilitates the integration of the five elements within the soul. Upon physical death, the elemental components of air, water, fire, and earth that comprise the human form disperse, initiating this reflective process as they reunite within the spiritual realm.

As part of the life review, individuals witness how their choices affected those around them and gain insights into why they chose specific paths. They also understand the broader narrative of their lives, recognizing the presence of spiritual guides, angels, and other beings throughout their journey. This perspective transcends the limitations of human consciousness, offering a higher understanding of their experiences. This allows individuals to review their lives spiritually, gaining clarity and perception beyond human comprehension. Additionally, the symbolic book of life, bearing the original name of your "Oversoul" at the time of incarnation, represents one's life journey.

Your Soul's Original Name/Sound

Discovering our Soul/Oversoul spiritual name is believed to reveal the original name given to us from the beginning of time, and it can be uncovered in this lifetime. These techniques are currently practiced here on Earth and involve calculating astrological charts. However, more than a regular reading will be required; a specialized chart reading is required. In this process, the degrees of the Zodiacal wheel are converted into letters, and specific alignments are interpreted to unveil a soul name that can awaken the individual's higher self. Accuracy in birth times is crucial for this calculation, and only a few highly experienced astrologers possess the knowledge to perform this technique. Despite its exclusivity, the quest to know one's original soul name is gaining popularity. Additionally, each soul is believed to have an original song or sound that emanates when it fluctuates, and other souls can hear it in the higher realms. This ethereal sound resembles the majestic communication of whales and dolphins.

SOUND TIP: Get a 528 hertz sound tuning fork to focus energy and balance your body through this sound frequency.

Life Review (continues)

As individuals transition into the life review, their spiritual guides provide support, healing, and guidance. This transformative process involves witnessing and understanding the impact of negative and positive actions, promoting healing and forgiveness. It also allows reflection on the meaningful contributions and love shared with others, evoking powerful emotions that transcend human description. Moreover, the life review serves as a platform for continued spiritual growth and learning, providing individuals with opportunities for healing and education based on their life experiences. It is a profound journey that encompasses the interconnectedness of all life and offers the potential for personal and spiritual development beyond physical existence. All of this is filled with the utmost love and respect for the journey, and of course, the forgiveness is unexplainable. It becomes clear that everything that happened to us was for us to grow. The more depths of despair, pain, and experience we had to go through, the more we have learned.

Week 6. Day 5 – The Akashic Records, The Halls of Learning, and The Cherubim Chamber

Within each of us lies a unique spiritual repository housing a wealth of knowledge, stories, and truths — the Akashic Records. This ethereal library encapsulates our journey and contains the records of our existence. Although our earthly minds tend to gravitate towards tangible, physical concepts, it's essential to recognize that these spiritual archives exist beyond the confines of the physical realm. They're a personalized dimension of consciousness, exclusively yours, storing the vibrational imprint of your being. Isn't that exciting! You can even design it to look how you want through your energy just by thinking of it or dreaming about it. I wish I could show everyone their records so they could get excited about their being and vibration. You will never look at yourself or life the same again once you see, feel, or hear who you are at this level.

Think of it as a sanctuary filled with your energy, experiences, and narratives — a place where the book of your life is archived after each life review, ready for you to revisit and study at any moment. This presence serves as a healing force, offering insight into the essence of who you are. The records never intrude upon us; they adapt to meet our needs. If visualizing this repository as a serene garden, a tranquil pool, or a lush rose garden makes it feel more accessible and relatable to you, embrace that visualization.

By acknowledging the existence of these records and understanding their significance, a profound shift occurs within our spirits. This awareness marks the beginning of a deeper understanding of our identity. We start to comprehend the importance and value of each soul, recognizing it as a precious and miraculous entity deserving of protection at all costs. This awakening leads to a powerful alignment with our true selves, fostering a newfound appreciation for the intricate beauty of our souls.

The Halls of Learning are the same thing, but for the entire Planet Earth, the Universe it's in ... and beyond. It houses a copy of every record from everywhere from all time. Could you imagine what that might look like if it was physical? There are record keepers there, and if you can get into enough of a trance when you meditate, you can go in and ask anything you want or need. Many famous people have been known to connect with the Halls of Records to create their co-created masterpieces, including musicians like Beethoven and inventors like Tesla. Of course, this is my opinion here and cannot be factually verified, but I do know that consciousness helps us create items to help the world. Even social media was partly made through spirit because we needed ways to spread messages worldwide faster. Of course, even a positive has a negative, just like every piece of light has a dark side.

The Cherubim Chamber

I detailed in the book's preface the concept that everything, including life itself, is in constant motion and must be updated regularly. This idea explains why many people are turning away from strict religious beliefs, as they realize that we are constantly evolving beings of energy. It no longer feels right to impose rigid limitations on ourselves. It's a belief that such restrictions were not intended to be in place indefinitely, but rather were established for individuals or souls who have caused significant harm to the planet. There is limited information available about this chamber, but it is said to be intended for those who have committed atrocious acts against humans, animals, or the environment. It is believed that this concept originated with the passing of Hitler, who was reportedly the first to be placed in the Cherubim Chamber. However, this is an evolving concept that may be revised in the future. It is suggested that even though the consciousness of Hitler is accessible in the Halls of Records as part of our history, some souls become so dark that they are beyond redemption. It is akin to a form of retirement, preventing them from returning to physical existence. According to this belief, after undergoing a Life Review, these souls are led to an additional room and placed in a pool of milky substance. Cherubim creatures then fly around the soul in the pool, showing them the horrific things they have done in their lives, causing harm to other living beings. The souls are made to experience the suffering they caused others fully. Eventually, they can return to a state of love, just like all other souls. However, some souls are not permitted to reincarnate due to the severity of their actions during their time on Earth.

Going to the Akashic Records for Exploration

Meditation. Please do The Liberated Healer grounding meditation, Earth & Cosmic, Golden Suns, and Protection for 20 minutes before this work. Put on calming music if that helps you to get into a great practice. Let it all flow through you.

Opening the Akashic Records Prayer

May it be with the blessings of Source Light that this journey helps us to connect all of ourselves. So, we do acknowledge the Forces of Light,

Asking for guidance, direction, and courage to know the Truth.

It is revealed for our highest good and the highest good of everyone connected to us.

Protect me from self-centeredness and direct my attention to the work at hand.

Help me to know myself ________________ (say your full name three times; you can even add your birthday to connect to your records) in the Light of the Akashic Records,

To see myself/or someone else's name if you are reading others ________________ (say your full name three times).

Through the eyes of the Lords and the Ambassadors of the Records, please enable me to share the wisdom and compassion that the Masters, Teachers, and Loved Ones of (say your name here) have for (say your name here or the person you are opening the records for here).

The Records are now open.
The Records are now open.
The Records are now open.

Reading the Akashic Records

While in a meditative state, imagine being able to see your records. Once you have the image in your mind, imagine grounding the records deep into the core of the Earth. Envision surrounding the records with a shining Golden Sun for healing. You can also offer the golden energy to the Source or the Supreme Being for additional healing. Utilize any tools you have learned here to help yourself, your surroundings, or anything encountered in your Akashic Records. It may take time to fully believe in what you are experiencing through sight, sound, or knowing. Don't force anything; if you encounter resistance, it might indicate underlying fear. Take a break and return another day. Remember, you are in control. Proceed when you feel ready, and take a break if things become overwhelming. Although you may encounter some sad stuff, the Akashic Records is a place of light and love, so it shouldn't become too overwhelming. It's also where we delve deep into past life readings for you and others in your soul group. Enjoy the process!

What does it look like? Is there a guard staring at a watch? What do they look like? What kinds of clothes are they wearing? Is there water, roses, or a garden? Please describe or draw.

____

____

Your Akashic Records from the Outside

Use this frame to draw anything you are seeing.

Walk into the building, and you should see rows and rows of books on shelves like an old-timey library with ladders to get to all the books. You might even see an additional librarian here who is an expert on you. Please describe what you are seeing.

Your Akashic Records from the Inside

Use this frame to draw anything you are seeing.

Travel to one of the books (we recommend only processing a few lives or questions simultaneously). If you want, you can use your pendulum to get answers to yes and no questions, which can be easier for some. Here are some questions and things you can do to start:

- Who are you at the core?
- Where were you originally conceived?
- Who are you to eventually become?
- What are some of the soul's core wounds?
- Have you traveled with a specific person before, and how many times (you can use the spiritual gauge for this one if you need a number)?
- You can bring up a situation you are going through now and ask the Master how this thing that happened for you is helping. You can ask them for help healing from the situation.

- You can even take a book of a life that you get to read, go through it, and write down what you hear, see, and feel from that life. You can also give that life a Golden Sun and some energy or surround it with love.
- You can look at old patterns and archetypes and see when and where you repeatedly played them. Once you see a pattern, it will help you uncover who you are and why you make confident choices.
- How is this assisting me?
- If an old version comes out that you see and it needs healing, give yourself one in that version of you. Surround it in love, validate it: "I am sorry you had to go through that; of course, you are upset; I love you." As you do this, the distress will start to fall away.
- How do I fall in love with life more?
- Why am I here this time around? What is my central theme here?
- Show me another past life where this happened ________.

Please note your experiences and past lives here; it'll be fun to reexamine them later.

____

____

____

____

____

____

Closing the Akashic Records Prayer – make sure you close the records

Thank you, I love you, and I would like to thank the Masters, Teachers, and Loved Ones for their love and compassion. I want to thank the Lords of the Akashic Records for their viewpoint of the records of (insert the name of the person you read here).

And I would like to thank the Holy Spirit of Light for all knowledge and healing.

The Records are now closed. Amen.
The Records are now closed. Amen.
The Records are now closed. Amen.

Week 6. Day 6 – Soul of Earth, Cities, Animals, Sea Creatures, Plants, the Oceans, and Mountains

The World Needs You: A Reason to Stay

As our time in this program draws to a close, I sincerely hope you've experienced profound realizations and growth and, most importantly, recognized and embraced your unique qualities. Acknowledging the abundance of wonder and magic that surrounds us is essential. While we've primarily focused on the human experience, understanding our individuality can lead to recognizing the interconnectedness of all our experiences.

Not only does Earth possess a soul and a unique vibration, but it also maintains an Akashic Record and a profound desire for existence. Similarly, continents, countries, states, cities, and towns all possess their distinctive soul, vibration, Akashic Record, and yearning for life. Delving into a city's official incorporation date allows us to glean insights, and applying astrology enables us to uncover the elemental vibrations of Earth, Fire, Water, and Air in a specific location.

Animals, sea creatures, and insects reflect the interconnectedness of all living beings. It suggests that animals and insects have souls characterized by the beauty and harmony of light and dark. Animals have a purity of spirit, and harming them disrupts that purity. It also mentions a personal anecdote about communicating with a ladybug, highlighting the belief in all living beings' profound wisdom and ancient nature. The text ultimately encourages heightened awareness and appreciation for the magic and interconnectedness of life.

The ocean, rivers, lakes, crystals, plants, trees, shrubs, mountains, rocks, and items in and around your home have living energy that needs healing, love, and energy like everything else.

The Earth is entering a new phase of its existence, and many people have noticed significant changes in the weather and natural events, with more expected to come. This is a natural part of the Earth's cycle; we are merely along for the journey. It's awe-inspiring to think about how this incredible planet was formed through the birth of celestial bodies and the accumulation of plasma, bacteria, and energy, ultimately giving rise to the remarkable human race. Despite the Earth's nurturing nature and boundless love for us, we, as a species, have caused great harm to her. Our actions have led to the upheaval of the natural world and even the creation of devastating conflicts like wars. In times of turmoil, we call upon the spiritual realm for assistance, and while angels and ancestors strive to aid us, there are limitations to what they can do. It's a sobering reminder that we can shape the physical world and bear responsibility for our actions.

Humanity's way of life often involves dwelling on the past and worrying about the future, unlike other Earth animals that live in the moment. Many believe they are superior to other living creatures because they are concerned with past influences and future projections. They create laws and rules to control these worries, unlike other animals that trust their inner guidance and live based on their instincts.

Humans often fear death and strive to hold on to life for as long as possible, which prevents them from fully experiencing all that life has to offer. This fear of death and the tendency to cling to past traumas trap the soul, preventing it from moving forward and experiencing new things.

Individuals must let go of their past ties and trust the universe to lead them. By living in the moment and relinquishing fears about the future, people can live freely and experience happiness and abundance. This is crucial not only for their well-being but also for the planet's well-being.

Earth itself has fears and calls for help from its inhabitants. Humans must heed this call, not only for themselves but also for the sake of the planet and all its living beings. Connecting with the Earth and embracing our differences can create new communities that honor and support one another, contributing to a balanced and harmonious world.

Embracing the uniqueness of each individual and working together to support one another can make Earth an extraordinary place in the universe, full of diversity and life.

Week 6. Day 7 – Sharing, Being "In-Service" with Your Full Passions or Creativity, Final Notes

You have now completed the *Handbook for the Living*. Please mark this day here with some of your parting ideas and how you want to move forward.

____

____

____

____

______

______

______

______

Passion for Change – Being In-Service

It's lovely to have a deep passion for causing positive change in something you genuinely believe in. Whether it's advocating for humans, animals, or the environment, your desire to make a difference is commendable. However, it's important to approach this with love to create real and lasting change. When you express yourself with anger, hostility, or insults, you not only hinder progress but also carry these negative energies, affecting yourself and those around you.

Schools should be safe havens for our children, and no one should feel afraid to seek an education. When conducting protests or advocating for change, you must ensure that you don't alienate others or create fear. By promoting love and self-healing, we can work towards ending conflicts caused by human actions.

Nobody appreciates being judged or dictated to. Practicing less judgment benefits individuals and has a positive impact on the world.

After focusing on your healing journey, find your unique way to contribute to the world and your local community. You can inspire others and drive positive change by demonstrating the transformative power of healing. Ultimately, as members of this planet, we are all on this journey together. I'm grateful to have you as part of this journey, and I'm excited to witness the progress you'll make in your life and the lives of those around you. Thank you for being part of this shared experience. I can't express enough in English my love for you!

Next Steps

Please take the next six weeks to completely internalize and apply everything you have learned, mastering the tools until they become ingrained in your very being. The ideal state is achieving unity of mind, body, spirit, and soul, creating a harmonious whole within yourself. This integration will allow you to navigate life's challenges more fluidly as you work on your personal growth and savor your experiences. Understanding the process of transitioning from this life should also help alleviate the fear of your eventual passing. Even if you doubt or question some of the concepts presented, the critical thing is whether you feel better and love yourself more. The goal is to live a purpose-driven life, waking up each day filled with excitement and purpose, knowing that your actions positively impact the world around you. You will become kinder to yourself, others, animals, and the planet through this journey. Although life may present challenges, the key is to navigate through them, and all the tools provided are here to support you on this journey.

Food/Exercise – Healing Your Temple

As you do this work, you will naturally want to start eating better and exercising as you fall more in love with yourself. You will feel the energy of the food and how it was cared for. You will become more sensitive and able to taste or know foods with chemicals in or on them. The impact of ingesting synthetic or non-natural food preservatives may manifest as discomfort in the stomach. It is essential to heed your instincts and pay attention to the messages your surroundings are conveying. My recovery from Myalgic Encephalomyelitis (ME)/chronic fatigue syndrome (CFS) was influenced by spiritual practices and mindful dietary choices. Nurturing my body became an intrinsic part of my spiritual journey. Self-love played a significant role in this process, making it more profound.

My susceptibility to illness has significantly decreased, and if I do fall ill, the duration is brief. My body efficiently processes anything it encounters. This is particularly remarkable given my previous struggle with chronic fatigue syndrome/ME healing involved consuming the right foods and adopting an active lifestyle. However, I am convinced that the transformation in my energy field was pivotal. Our physical well-being is intertwined with the energy that surrounds us. *The Hidden Messages in Water* by Masaru Emoto was a valuable resource for me. Emoto's best-selling book delves into the impact of our thoughts, words, and emotions on water molecules, illustrating their potential to influence the Earth and human health positively. (Emoto, 2005, p. 7)

Being Sexually Intimate

When we connect intimately with others, our energies intertwine in various ways — understanding how to clear these energies after each interaction is essential to maintaining our vibration. If you find yourself feeling different after spending a lot of time with someone who has a prominent illness or mental health issue, you might be inadvertently taking on some of their traits to heal them. However, there are more effective ways to help them than this self-sacrifice. It's essential to cleanse yourself using the spiritual techniques described in this book. While absorbing dark and light energies from others is possible, you can return to your natural state by grounding yourself, running your energy, and establishing protective barriers. Releasing others' energies doesn't diminish your love for them or disconnect you from them — it simply resets you to your natural vibration.

Dimensions and Timelines

I've been instructed to refrain from diving into the dimension topic extensively. However, it's important to express that dimensions are conscious levels rather than physical places. Transitioning between dimensions is a conscious process, not a physical one. The Earth plane, known as the third dimension, is where souls work through their karma and is characterized by density. On the other hand, the fifth dimension is where beings who have attained a certain level of spiritual development resonate consciously. Moving between the third and fifth dimensions of your personal growth is possible. Still, the aim is to remain in the fifth dimension as much as possible to experience the highest love vibration. Instead of getting too caught up in ascending into different dimensions, focusing on staying in the energy of love and following what excites you the most can be more beneficial for most people.

Sleeping Spirits/Rebuilding from The Past

Many souls on this planet are in a deep slumber and are only experiencing the density of the lower levels and the third dimension. This is where they belong, and it is up to them to shift. The best way to do this is to raise your frequency, and they shall follow through with your example. It is not for us to judge people by elevation. That takes out of the world we are trying to create. A lot of souls are sucked into addictions, darker activities such as hurting animals, children, or the elderly, and consuming drugs that are lowering their vibrations and hurting their temple and the Planet (this includes alcohol, too much refined sugars, and some medications). It is painful for society to watch, and creating programs to help those who carry these afflictions in their being is necessary to continue. We need to help bring them out of the shadows. It's hard because the level of anger when you see someone doing something so vile can and will take you over. Anger only brings in more anger; the

Planet has so much money for things that are not helpful. We need healthcare to be better in all categories to win. We need the wealthy to wake up and see that some of their single activities can feed a country. Save children. If you don't do this for yourself, let's do it for the voiceless, like the animals, children, and elderly.

We can and should be a better society. There is a right way to treat all living creatures and a despicable way. We cannot sweep this under the rug anymore. To heal us all, we need to go back to the early traditions like the tribes that were ushered away, like the "Trail of Tears," where over 20,000 Native Americans were demanded to leave their homes, signed by Andrew Jackson, the USA's then-president (Ehle, n.d.).That energy created a dark moment for the country and created systematic karma. We can heal it. Go back to love, kindness, prayer, and ritual for all. Ask forgiveness for all the wrongs that our ancestors have done, and many of the souls here today are a part of the good, bad, and the ugly. We are those souls from all sides. Again, we have all played terrible roles. I should also mention what was done about the slave trade in America. What kind of pain and karma do you think it brought? Recognize the shamefulness of those acts and help everyone heal. No wonder there was so much pain. If you hate one race that much, guess what race you will most likely become in the next life? That is how it works; it would be best if we just accepted everyone where they are right now and worked it out!

*I live in Southern California. As I started to write about the "Trail of Tears," the blue skies changed, and clouds rolled in. Now, it is pouring rain in the middle of summer. To me, this is spirit giving a thank you of acknowledgment. If you have ever been a part of a big ceremony, especially with a shaman, you will see shifts happen like this: the spirit is miraculous. I also want to note that I have been working with Chief Yonaguska

(Yonaguska, n.d.), who came in through a client to help clear this karma. It's been some of my most rewarding work. I have a little Cherokee blood inside of me that I confirmed through DNA tests. I have always been drawn to them.

It's important to acknowledge that many individuals on this Earth are unaware and have a lower consciousness. Those of us who have awakened to higher frequencies have a responsibility to lead by example and inspire others to elevate their vibrations. Rather than passing judgment on others, we should strive to create a world of compassion and understanding. Many people are suffering from addictions and engaging in harmful behaviors that lower their energy and impact both themselves and the planet. It's painful to witness, and we must implement programs to support those struggling and bring them out of the darkness. We must resist succumbing to anger when confronted with such negativity, as anger only perpetuates more negativity. Redirecting resources to improve healthcare and addressing societal issues is essential for progress. We should all strive for a society that values and respects all living beings. To heal and move forward, we need to draw from ancient traditions and seek forgiveness for the wrongdoings of our ancestors. We're all connected to human history's good, bad, and ugly, and it's crucial to acknowledge and heal from this collective past. It's also important to address the painful legacy of historical events such as the Trail of Tears and the slave trade and work towards healing the wounds caused by these injustices. Finally, we should aim to break the cycle of karmic suffering and strive for forgiveness and understanding for ourselves and others.

In reflecting on my past lives, I have encountered instances that filled me with pride and others that evoked disappointment. One vivid recollection was of a life as a French Commander during WWI, where I harbored deep regret for my cruel actions. It was difficult to confront this realization, yet I strive not to dwell on past horrors. Instead, I seek forgiveness for myself and extend it to those I have wronged. We are caught in a cycle of inflicting new wounds and perpetuating hurt, and we must break free from this cycle of karmic retribution.

Volume 2 – Thank You

Volume 2 will be needed to explain the advanced techniques for *Planet Walking*. Although these lessons have not been fully downloaded or even described to me yet, I am still actively learning them, and I hope you will continue this journey with me (us). This has been a rewarding experience, and we are so excited and grateful to know each of you. We wish you well in your learning and hope you are filled with love and joy.

Resources

Here is a list of resources we recommend that go deeper into the mentioned categories.

Crisis Lifelines

Nine hundred eleven (911) for any emergency in the United States of America and immediate medical assistance for ambulance transport to a hospital. If you are having suicidal thoughts, it might be better to look at the options below with people trained in listening to your specific needs. You don't have to be suicidal to use these lines; you can call them if you just need an empathetic ear or to ask what you can do to help someone else.

988 and **1-800-SUICIDE** (1-800-784-2433): The National Hope Line Network will connect you with a counselor based on your area code; push 1 for Veterans or text 838255; press 2 for LGBTQA+; and TTY users, use your preferred relay service or dial 711. Chat at 988lifeline.org.

Canada Kids Help: 1-800-668-6868 and Parents Hotline: 1-888-603-9100 offer bilingual, anonymous phone counseling and referral services to children.

CDC National HIV and AIDS Hotline: 1-800-232-4636.

Center for Elderly Suicide Prevention (CESP) Friendship Line: 1-800-971-0016 (ioaging.org). This is a 24/7 hotline for seniors, family members, caregivers, and advocates.

Childhelp National Child Abuse Hotline: Call or text 1-800-422-4453. For issues related to child abuse, Childhelp connects you with professional counselors to help in a crisis and provides information on how to get help. They offer phone support in 170 languages, or you can chat online with a counselor.

Cop 2 Cop: 1-866-267-2267 (cop2coponline.org). 24/7 assistance from law enforcement offices.

Covenant House Nineline: 1-800-999-9999 (covenanthouse.org). This organization provides crisis intervention, referral, and information services to troubled youth and their families.

Crisis Text Line: Text HOME to USA/741741, SHOUT to UK/85258, or CONNECT to Canada/686868. Use phone, WhatsApp, or Facebook. Crisis Text Line fields messages about suicidal thoughts, abuse, sexual assault, depression, anxiety, bullying, and more. Its uniqueness is that it's entirely text-based, which makes it easy for anyone who doesn't feel comfortable or safe talking on the phone to use it.

Girls and Boys Town National Hotline: 1-800-448-3000 in English/Spanish (girlsandboystown.org/). Serving children and families in a variety of ways.

LGBTA+ Senior Hotline: 1-888-234-7243.

LGBTQA+ National Hotline: 1-888-843-4564.

National Domestic Violence Hotline: Text START to 88788 or call 1-800-799-7233.

National Hopeline Network: 1-800-784-2433.

National Resource Center for Suicide Prevention and Aftercare: 1-770-541-1114.

National Sexual Assault Hotline: 1-800-656-4673.

National Suicide Prevention Lifeline: 1-800-273-8255.

Not My Kid, Inc.: 1-602-652-0163.

RAINN: 1-800-656-4673. The Rape, Abuse & Incest National Network's hotline is for anyone who has experienced sexual abuse or assault. When you call its central hotline, you'll be connected with someone at a local organization in your area who can provide live support and direct you to additional resources. RAINN also offers live chat on its website.

Special Interest Book Recommendations

Angels: The Definitive Guide to Angels from Around the World by Marie-Ange Faugerolas

Animal Spirit Guides: An Easy-to-Use Handbook for Identifying and Understanding Your Power Animals and Animal Spirit Helpers by Steven D. Farmer

Astrology's Magical Nodes of the Moon by Carmen Turner-Schott

The Atlas of Mind, Body and Spirit by Paul Hougham

Autobiography of a Yogi by Paramahansa Yogananda

Awakening to the Fifth Dimension by Kimberly Meredith

The Body Keeps the Score: Brain, Mind, and Body in the Healing of Trauma by Bessel van der Kolk

Care of the Soul by Thomas Moore

The Cross and the Lynching Tree by James H. Cone

Earthing by Clinton Ober, Stephen T. Sinatra, MD, and Martin Zucker

Embrace Your Empathy by Kristy Robinett

Encyclopedia of Spirits: The Ultimate Guide to the Magic of Fairies, Genies, Demons, Ghosts, Gods & Goddesses by Judika Illes

Healing Through the Akashic Records by Linda Howe

The Hidden Power of Aikido by Susan Perry, PhD

The Highly Sensitive Person's Guide to Dealing with Toxic People: How to Reclaim Your Power from Narcissists and Other Manipulators by Shahida Arabi

The Journey from Abandonment to Healing: Surviving Through and Recovering from the Five Stages that Accompany the Loss of Love by Susan Anderson

The Keepers of the Light Codes by Rhiannon Heins

Liberating Jesus by Roberta Grimes

The Lives of Angels by Emanuel Swedenborg

Many Lives, Many Masters: The True Story of a Prominent Psychiatrist, His Young Patient, and the Past-Life Therapy That Changed Both Their Lives by Brian Weiss, MD

May the Love Force Be With You by Joni Dittrich, PhD (Rajashree Maa)

The Mystery of Life Energy: Biofield Healing, Phantom Limbs, Group Energetics, and Gaia Consciousness by Eric Leskowitz, MD

No Bad Parts: Healing Trauma & Restoring Wholeness with The Internal Family Systems Model by Richard Schwartz

On Death and Dying by Elisabeth Kübler-Ross, MD

On Grief and Grieving: Finding the Meaning of Grief Through the Five Stages of Loss by Elisabeth Kübler-Ross, MD

Peace Is Every Step: The Path of Mindfulness in Everyday Life by Thich Nhat Hanh

Pendulums & Intuition: Practical Advice for Trusting Your Inner Wisdom by Karina Muller and Lana Gendlin

The Persistence of the Soul: Mediums, Spirit Visitations, and the Afterlife Communication by Mark Ireland

The Prophet by Kahlil Gibran

Rest Is Resistance: A Manifesto by Tricia Hersey

The Rise and Fall of Britain's Best Psychic Medium by Nicky Alan

Sacred Contracts by Caroline Myss

Stillness Speaks by Eckhart Tolle, Author of *The Power of Now*

Unlock the Power of Your Chakras: An Immersive Experience through Exercises, Yoga Sets & Meditations by Masuda Mohamadi

Where Do We Go from Here by Martin Luther King, Jr.

The Wild Unknown Archetypes Deck and Guidebook by Kim Krans

You Are Psychic: The Art of Clairvoyant Reading and Healing by Debra Lynne Katz

Online Program

The Anxious Calm with Figgi Life – Dr. Jeanne Retief. The Anxious Calm is an online program where anyone struggling

with anxiety can learn how to peacefully coexist with their unique wiring to thrive in an anxious world. This sacred space connects you to those who understand the anxious path: access valuable resources and the tools you need to discover the hidden gifts of your anxiety. Find support in a space where it's okay, NOT be okay, and never feel isolated again. Blessed are those who learn to fly. https://www.docjeanne.com/

Bibliography

Anka, Darryl. *The Masters of Limitation: An ET's Observations of Earth*. Darryl Anka Publishing, May 2020.

Website: https://www.bashar.org/fivelaws

Emoto, Masaru. *The Hidden Messages in Water*. Atria Books, 7, 2005, 2011.

Website: https://books.google.com/books?id=kb4mcLF7WHc-C&dq=messages+in+water+book&lr=&source=gbs_navl

Minges, P. "Beneath the Underdog: Race, Religion, and the Trail of Tears." *American Indian Quarterly*, Volume 25, Number 3. University of Nebraska Press, 2001.

Biography

Gina Cavalier Bio

Gina Cavalier is a multi-talented individual who wears many hats — she is an author, writer, artist, public speaker, executive producer at Love and Media, and Founder of The Liberated Healer. Gina is dedicated to using various forms of media, such as books, programs, documentaries, mobile apps, and support groups, to address the most pressing issues facing humanity. Her mission is to inspire and support people through diverse storytelling, ultimately aiming to impact the world positively.

Cavalier is a media veteran, former entertainment studio executive, and technology enthusiast. She has contributed to over three hundred film/TV titles, such as the *Harry Potter* and *Fantastic Beasts and Where to Find Them* franchises. Cavalier began her speaking career at Warner Bros. Studio, where she established a business resource group that organized insightful events for over 600 attendees. She now speaks to teams at corporations, schools, bookstores, veterans' meetings, and conferences.

Cavalier's first published book is ***Surviving Suicidal Ideation: From Therapy to Spirituality and the Lived Experience,*** which she has coauthored with a trauma-informed therapist, Dr. Amelia Kelley, with 30 hand-inked illustrations by Cavalier, published by The Swedenborg Foundation in 2024. The Foreword is by Thomas Moore, the acclaimed spiritual author of *Care of the Soul*. The book shares her biography tale and profound journey through healing her suicidal ideation.

www.TheLiberatedHealer.com
www.GinaCavalier.com
www.LoveandMedia.com

Thank you for connecting to Planet Walking, A Handbook for the Living. I hope you found some nuggets of inspiring messages and hope. If you feel compelled, please leave a review at the bookstore where you purchased it, as it helps to continue the messages. Don't hesitate to contact me with any comments or questions at gigicavalier@gmail.com.

O-BOOKS

SPIRITUALITY

O is a symbol of the world, of oneness and unity; this eye represents knowledge and insight. We publish titles on general spirituality and living a spiritual life. We aim to inform and help you on your own journey in this life.
If you have enjoyed this book, why not tell other readers by posting a review on your preferred book site?

Recent bestsellers from O-Books are:

Awakening Child
A journey of inner transformation through teaching your child mindfulness and compassion.
Heather Grace MacKenzie
Paperback: 978-1-78535-408-3 ebook: 978-1-78535-409-0

A Colourful Dose of Optimism
Prescribe your own Happy Colours to Feel Good NOW
Jules Standish
It's time for us to look on the bright side, by boosting our mood and lifting our spirit, both in our interiors, as well as our closet.
Paperback: 978-1-78904-927-5 ebook: 978-1-78904-928-2

Natural Happiness

Use Organic Gardening Skills to Cultivate Yourself

Alan Heeks

Deepen your roots to grow through uncertainty.

Paperback: 978-1-80341-496-6 ebook: 978-1-80341-497-3

Daylight Saving Time

The Power of Growing Older

David W. Berner

Daylight Saving Time: Facing age with grace and mindfulness.

Paperback: 978-1-80341-511-6 ebook: 978-1-80341-520-8

Generation Panic

Simple & Empowering Techniques to Combat Anxiety

Agi Heale

Generation Panic is a one-stop shop with over 100 tips and techniques to help busy professionals combat anxiety.

Paperback: 978-1-78904-515-4 ebook: 978-1-78904-516-1

Life Before the Internet

What we can learn from the good old days

Michael Gentle

A fascinating look back at a slower, simpler time, when Amazon was just a river.

Paperback: 978-1-80341-388-4 ebook: 978-1-80341-389-1

Breath for Health

A Mindful Way to Restore Your Natural Breathing Cycle

Michael D Hutchinson

Discover the secrets hidden in yoga and modern physiology — and restore your natural, healthy, confident way of breathing in just 10 minutes a day.

Paperback: 978-1-80341-440-9 ebook: 978-1-80341-441-6

Readers of ebooks can buy or view any of these bestsellers by clicking on the live link in the title. Most titles are published in paperback and as an ebook. Paperbacks are available in traditional bookshops. Both print and ebook formats are available online.

Find more titles and sign up to our readers' newsletter at **www.o-books.com**

Follow O-Books on Facebook at **O-Books**